BOARDING THE
WESTBOUND

BOARDING THE
WESTBOUND

Journey of a Depression-era Hobo

Joseph Szalanski

WORD ASSOCIATION PUBLISHERS
www.wordassociation.com
1.800.827.7903

Copyright © 2010 by Joseph Szalanski

All Rights reserved. No part of this publication may be reproduced, stored in a retrieval system or transmitted, in any form or by any means, electronic, mechanical, photocopying, recording, or otherwise, without the prior written permission of the publisher.

Printed in the United States of America.

Cover photograph courtesy of The Salvation Army National Archives.

ISBN: 978-1-59571-487-9

Library of Congress Control Number: 2009942296

Designed and published by

Word Association Publishers
205 Fifth Avenue
Tarentum, Pennsylvania 15084

www.wordassociation.com
1.800.827.7903

DEDICATION

To my father and mother
Joseph F. and Louise DeMichele Szalanski

Contents

Introduction xi

Chapter 1
The Accident 17

Chapter 2
Immigrating from Europe 29

Chapter 3
America in the 1920s 43

Chapter 4
Hard Times 59

Chapter 5
Hobo Culture 67

Chapter 6
Joe Becomes a Hobo 79

Chapter 7
Getting Fed on the Road 85

Chapter 8
Places to Sleep 119

Chapter 9
Railroad Bulls 133

Chapter 10
Looking Like a Hobo 145

Chapter 11
Entertainment 163

Chapter 12
Four Cities, One Desert 181

Chapter 13
Holidays 201

Chapter 14
Admiring the Views 209

Chapter 15
Returning Home 217

Chapter 16
A Wife's Memories 225

Appendix I
Hobo Glossary 237

Appendix II
Trip Details 241

Appendix III
Joe's Journal 253

Acknowledgments 281

Bibliography 285

About the Author
Joseph Szalanski 289

INTRODUCTION

My father was killed in a steel mill accident when I was two months old, so I have no conscious awareness or memories of him. I do have a treasure of stories told of him and his life, the pre-eminent being his excursion through the country by hopping freights during the Depression. He did this as a twenty-two year old and, fortunately, had the foresight and determination to keep a daily diary chronicling the events of his months on the road. The paper and penciled writing are still remarkably well preserved, and the quality of the writing is impressive, especially for a man with an eighth grade education who was raised by parents whose native tongue was Polish.

These diaries are used as the basis for this book, and to give them context and perspective, I have recalled some family history and several defining events of the early twentieth century. I don't purport to give a thorough, scholarly examination of the era, but believe that a minimal familiarity is necessary to help understand various social and economic environments of the first four decades of the last century.

Emphasis is given to the viewpoint of the immigrants from Eastern and Southern Europe who were welcomed by captains of industry as a source of ample and inexpensive labor, but who encountered hostility from the entrenched Anglo Saxons concerned about the possible effects these predominately Catholic newcomers would have on the country's culture.

I have an especial fondness for these immigrants, having been raised in a household that included my maternal grandmother and a great uncle, both of whom came from Italy. The vast majority of newcomers harbored no illusions that the world was created for their pleasure, yet never seemed to be deficient in happy, loving moments.

The new immigrants focused primarily on providing expanded economic and educational opportunities for their children and succeeding generations, and raised their children to become quickly immersed in the dominant American culture, doing this so well that these children became an integral part of what is now called America's Greatest Generation.

My father took becoming Americanized to another level, traveling to every one of the forty-eight states that comprised 1932 America, mentioning at least one locale in each state in his diary. This book does not reprint the diary in its entirety, but rather uses excerpts to illustrate various facets of everyday hobo life and to relate many of the unusual and amusing episodes in it. It was written in two notebooks, the first of which was mailed home when filled and with the added notation that he would give more details upon his return.

He did expound on his exploits to family and friends, and expressed a desire to write about them in later years, years never granted. I have endeavored to put much of it into print more than seventy-five years after it was written, without the additional details he would have provided, but with the benefit of history, to better understand the times in which he lived and rode.

Boarding the Westbound

CHAPTER 1
THE ACCIDENT

The Carnegie - Illinois Homestead Works alongside the
Monongohela River, later merged into US Steel.

Photograph courtesy of the Rivers of Steel National Heritage Area.

On March 8, 1940, the steel mills along the Monongahela River were working at full capacity. Huge plants in Braddock, Homestead, Duquesne, Clairton, and McKeesport, spewed smoke from their great smokestacks, and along with a new finishing mill in West Mifflin, welcomed tens of thousands of dedicated steelworkers into their facilities each workday. They were visible welcome signs that the country had finally emerged from the economic devastation and hopelessness of the Great Depression. The Depression, which began with the stock market collapse in October 1929, had diminished economic activity to such an extent that as late as 1939 some ten million Americans were still unemployed. But by early 1940, people were working again, and their spirits, gripped by fear and uncertainty for ten long years, were starting to rise. Paychecks were being cashed, and hope was being restored. The smoke and the constant stream of men passing in and out of the mills validated this optimism.

Many of the workers streaming into the plants were men who had formed part of the vast immigration from eastern and southern Europe during the early 1900s, men who were among the millions that left the poverty and meager opportunity in their homelands to come to America. America's expanding industries, including iron and steel and coal mining, faced a labor shortage, and large numbers of these new immigrants settled in Western Pennsylvania to take some of the most difficult jobs in the steel mills and coal mines. By 1940, many sons of these newcomers had joined their fathers in the region's mills and mines.

JOURNEY OF A DEPRESSION-ERA HOBO

Such was the case with the Szalanski family. Vincent, his wife, Stella, and their children Marta, Jean, and Joe, left what is now the western part of Poland in 1910, settling in East Vandergrift, Pennsylvania, about thirty-two miles northeast of Pittsburgh. Vincent was a blacksmith by trade, and landed a job with the American Sheet and Tin Plate Company, a Vandergrift plant which in 1907 had earned the designation as the world's largest sheet mill. By the time his son Joe was able to get a job there during the economic resurgence in 1939, the plant had become part of the Carnegie—Illinois Steel Corporation, later part of United States Steel.

Vandergrift Mill
Photograph courtesy of Victorian Vandergrift Museum and Historical Society.

BOARDING THE WESTBOUND

The Vandergrift facility became part of the Irvin Works in September 1939, and Joe and hundreds of others were transferred to the recently built plant in West Mifflin. Some of those who were transferred moved closer to the new facility, but Joe and most of the others stayed in Vandergrift and tolerated the daily fifty-six-mile round trip. The company initially provided bus service, but the men soon formed car pools for convenience. Among the daily commuters from Vandergrift were two brothers of Joe's wife, Louise—Nick and Joe DeMichele. The men formed a cohesive group, sharing a time-consuming drive and hard work. They blended well as the work was difficult and they had to rely on each other for job performance and safety. Congeniality among workers went a long way toward lightening the atmosphere in a demanding, unrelenting environment.

This new plant, located about thirteen miles from Pittsburgh on the west bank of the Monongahela River, began operations in December 1938. The huge complex covered fifty-one acres and was a finishing mill, processing steel made in other company facilities into coils and sheets to be shipped to customers. With no steel made at Irvin, the absence of the fiery open hearths and blast furnaces gave the appearance of a safer work environment, although the one hundred or so overhead cranes used to transport steel among various departments created a different sort of hazard.

Air view of the Carnegie-Illinois Steel Corporation's
Irvin Works by the Monongahela River.
Photograph courtesy of the Rivers of Steel National Heritage Area.

Joe worked in the slab yard. This was where steel first entered the plant in the form of twenty-foot long, six-inch thick slabs, each weighing up to twenty thousand pounds. These gigantic slabs, made and shipped by rail from nearby plants directly into the slab yard, were stored and prepared for crane transport to the hot mill, where the processing cycle began.

March 8, 1940 began as a day to be happy, with the country on the upswing, spring on the way, and a new baseball season beginning with stars like Joe DiMaggio, Ted Williams, and Bob Feller emerging. Baseball was the true national pastime of the era and Joe, like many immigrants' sons, embraced it. He was an announcer on the public address system for the local sandlot team in Vandergrift, and was an active participant in the animated baseball discussions at work that often carried over into the ride home. This day's ride home was nearing. The men, though physically tired, had lighter hearts as the end of their shift approached.

At four o'clock, thousands of men would exit the mills as thousands more poured in to begin the four o'clock to midnight shift. Those leaving looked forward to being with family and friends in more pleasant conditions. On this day, at 3:45, as usual, they would be physically and mentally preparing to go home. At 3:50 on this day, March 8, 1940, Joe Szalanski would be dead.

An overhead crane dropped a ten-ton steel slab on the spot where he was standing, brutally crushing him to death. Many of his co-workers went into shock. Most had never seen a person die, let alone in such a horrible manner. This was not only a gruesome death, it was the end to a life of a man they knew and cared about. There would be no lighthearted baseball talk on the way home tonight, only mournful silence coming from strong men shocked into grief.

Four o'clock on March 8 was still a happy time in East Vandergrift. A big house on McKinley Avenue was home to the people most important to Joe. He and his wife Louise and two-month old son were living there along with his parents, Stella and Vincent. As Joe's body was lying crushed and lifeless on the Irvin Works floor, his family was preparing his meal and anticipating his return.

When the news was tearfully delivered, everything else became irrelevant. Neighbors recall Stella shrieking on the back porch, while Louise and Vincent were shocked into uncontrollable tears and grief. The words that no parents should ever have to hear completely devastated them. Adjusting to the tragedy would be difficult. Vincent never recovered from losing his eldest son, and died seven months later at the age of fifty-seven. Stella suffered nerve problems the remainder of her life, dying in 1959 after moving to Florida in 1946 with her younger sons Matthew and Zigmund.

Louise was overwhelmed by an array of emotions—all bad. Sorrow and a deep sense of loss mixed with fear and apprehension at the responsibility of raising their two-month-old son. Louise had only an eighth grade education. As the oldest girl in a family of eight children, she had been needed at home to help with household chores, later working as a housekeeper for other families. She could count on little help from either corporate America or the government. There were no accidental death lawsuits in this era, no survivor benefits, and no workmen's compensation settlements. She received some corporate help for the burial and was left to find her own way.

The months immediately after Joe's death brought great difficulty, but after that catastrophe most things seemed mere nuisances. The first steps in redirecting her life were to reclaim her former job at Schenley Distillery, and to move back with her mother.

The Depression era had been especially difficult for the DeMichele family. Louise's father, Domenick, died of a stroke in 1929, leaving his wife, Angeline, and their eight children to pull through those trying times without him. With the older kids working where they could and support from some very concerned and generous godparents, they did surprisingly well. However, their perpetually shaky financial conditions finally grew too burdensome. By 1940, the three oldest boys had moved out to start their own families. Louise's job at Schenley and her youngest brother Albert's work in the mines enabled the family to sustain itself, but past obligations that accumulated during the lean years of the 1930s were insurmountable.

Four months after Louise buried her husband, her family's house was lost. In July 1940 the Westmoreland County Sheriff's Office conveyed the title of the DeMichele house to the Vandergrift Savings and Trust for the sum of $375.00. Louise, still numb over the loss of Joe, had endured another setback. But this one could be overcome. Three months later, in October, her brother Nick, now married and the father of a three year old daughter, acquired the necessary funds to get the property deeded back to the family.

Louise assumed ownership of the house and lived there until her death at the age of eighty-seven. Ironically, in the month she died, April 2002, a granite memorial listing the names and dates of those felled at work was placed near the front gate of the Irvin Works. The first name on it is Joseph Szalanski.

Memorial Monument at Irvin Works.
Photograph courtesy of the Local 2227 USW.

BOARDING THE WESTBOUND

Louise made the best of the situation. She raised and educated her son and kept her mother at home until Angeline died in 1982 at the age of ninety-four. She never remarried and kept the memory of Joe alive in her heart for as long as she lived. While Joe's death was premature, as the years went by and Louise grew further away from that awful moment of receiving the news, her memories grew sweeter. In her mind, Joe was a young man and would forever remain so.

The stories told about my father would always be stories of a young man. They told of a kind man with many friends and a quick-witted sense of humor, but the story most repeated was the result of his sense of adventure and curiosity. In 1932, in the midst of the Great Depression, Joe and a friend from East Vandergrift joined the large number of unemployed Americans who traveled the country by hopping freight cars. Some went looking for work, some were looking to escape bad situations, and some—like Joe and Kelly—just wanted adventure. Kelly got enough after traveling from Pennsylvania to Maine and all the way down to Florida. When the two were offered a ride home in a truck from Tampa, Florida, Kelly chose to take it; my father didn't. Joe had declared his intentions in a letter sent to a friend, written in Richmond after being on the road for about a month:

> *You can bet your pants I am not coming back before I make 48 states and Canada will be thrown in for good measure, this is number 12 and 36 more to go, first 8*

JOURNEY OF A DEPRESSION-ERA HOBO

were pretty tough and next 8 will be tough too. You sure are missing lots of fun.

He wrote that he wanted to travel to all forty-eight states of the continental United States, and he did so. His trip covered 13,776 miles in four months, from late July to early December 1932. Joe saw America from coast to coast, border to border. He saw its changing landscapes, the oceans, the mountains, the prairies, and the deserts, and met people from small towns, big cities, farms, and villages. He talked with everyone he met, from those living in abandoned boxcars to people living in grand houses.

Joe was twenty-two years old during his trip and he kept a daily diary, filling 264 pages in two four-by-six inch notebooks. When the first book was filled, he mailed it back to a friend in East Vandergrift with a note on the last page: "C.D.—Do not copy any of this cause it only contains briefs will enlargen when I get home." These "briefs" were actually detailed accounts of where he went, who he met, what he did, how he ate, and where he slept each day. Joe planned to write an account of his excursion, an adventure he referred to as "my Hobo trip of 1932" on the cover of his first notebook. He planned to do this when he retired.

CHAPTER 2
IMMIGRATING FROM EUROPE

Joe was born in this house and after his parents took him and his two sisters to the United States, the house remained in the family with his aunt and uncle, Salome and Joseph Klonowski.

Photograph courtesy of Sylvester Klonowski.

My father's long journey began in another country, on another continent. He was born on February 10, 1910 in the village of Izabelin, near the city of Konin, in what is now Poland. In 1910 Poland did not exist as a sovereign state. The territory that now comprises the country was divided among Germany, Russia, and Austria–Hungary, with Izabelin located in the section controlled by Germany. When Joe was born in 1910, the family already had two girls, Marta born in 1906 and Jean in 1908.

Joe's family lived on a parcel of land owned by a large property owner. His father, Vincent, farmed and provided blacksmith services for the owner and other farmers who worked the land of this and adjoining properties. In 1910, the Polish agriculture economy was in a depressed state, and more important to Vincent, the Germans were adopting the concept of universal military service, and beginning to draft men from the region. While the world was not yet at war (World War I would begin in 1914) Vincent knew that a draft-induced absence would cause economic hardship for his family, and he would miss his wife and young children. He began to consider migrating to America, as millions of Poles, mostly poor peasant farmers, had done for the last several decades.

America certainly offered economic opportunity, as letters received from those already there attested. Also, he would be far from the grasp of the German army. Still, it was not an easy choice to make. His and Stella's decision would drastically alter the course of their lives, and even more so the lives of their children, leaving an area where their families had lived for centuries. This was their heritage, their culture, their language, and their traditions. In that era, moving halfway around the world was a final good-bye. Those who left and those who remained would exist for each other only in memory, thoughts, and prayers, and through an occasional letter. No more being able to share in the joys of birth and sadness of death, no more weddings or holidays to celebrate together, no more comforting each other in bad times and laughing together in the good.

This house in Scorciosa was built on the site of the dwelling of Domenick, Angeline and son John left in 1909.

While Vincent and Stella, my paternal grandparents, were in Izabelin in late 1910 trying to decide upon the best option for their family, Domenick and Angeline DeMichele (my mother, Louise's, parents) had been in America for almost a year. They left the village of Scorciosa, near the Adriatic Sea in the Abruzzi region of Italy, in 1909 with their infant son, John. After two more sons, their daughter Louise was born in 1914, and it was she who would marry

BOARDING THE WESTBOUND

Joe Szalanski in 1939. The voyage was Angeline's second crossing of the ocean. In 1895, at age seven, she accompanied her parents to Brazil, where she and the family worked as migrants picking coffee beans. A favorite story enjoyed by the DeMichele family was of Angeline watching television in her later years and seeing commercials for a coffee company that showed people hand-picking only the finest coffee beans. A riled Angeline would rise in her chair and explain that anybody who did that would be whipped. Pickers were instructed to open their aprons under the branches and shake the tree so the beans fell into the apron. Too many beans missing the apron and falling onto the ground was another cause for whipping. Angeline had to be assured that somebody would write to the television station to inform the producers of this.

My grandmother's second trip across the Atlantic took her to America, with the DeMichele family initially settling in Duncannon, Pennsylvania, where Domenick found work with the Pennsylvania Railroad. Her family grew, with sons Nick born in 1911 and Joe in 1912. A friend from Scorciosa, Luigi DiPaolo, joined them there, as did Domenick's brother, Joe. However, the longing for his native land, which all immigrants had to deal with, was too much for Joe, and he returned to Italy to live out his life. This was not uncommon, but those who stayed were committed to the course, and at the end of their lives felt certain they chose the right path for themselves and their children.

Though some returned, the growing American industrial base continued to lure streams of immigrants to fill the labor shortage. In 1910, Vincent and Stella Szalanski decided that

America was the best place for them and made the decision to leave, sailing on November 1, 1910, from Germany on the *Grosser Kurfest*. My paternal grandparents, like almost all of the other new immigrants, actually knew very little about America. A majority of immigrants of this era came from eastern and southern Europe, and most were uneducated, illiterate peasants. They brought a willingness to work hard in exchange for greater opportunities for succeeding generations.

The ships from Europe brought them to various cities on our eastern seaboard—Boston, Baltimore, New York, Philadelphia—although some went to Canada where many newcomers remained as others filtered down to the United States. The destination most widely-associated with the immigration of this era was New York's Ellis Island, built in 1892 to process people who were being greeted by the Statue of Liberty in the harbor.

The following exhibit is a portion of a large spreadsheet that helped process immigrants who arrived at Ellis Island on October 20, 1923, a group that included Domenick's brother Tomaso, sister Rose DeMichele Caravaggio, and nephew Donato Caravaggio. These three new arrivals listed my grandfather's 409 Linden Street, Vandergrift, PA house as their destination in the column that required immigrants to declare where they were going in America. Tomaso identified Domenick as his brother, while Rose stated she was joining her husband Giuseppe Caravaggio, who was staying at the house while awaiting his wife and son. The Caravaggios moved into their own house, right next to that of Domenick's and Rose's sister Mary DeMichele Pocetti, both homes being within a hundred yards of where Domenick lived, affording each other some continuity, stability, and comfort in the new land.

Part of the 33 column form that immigration officials had to complete on each new arrival at Ellis Island.

Photograph courtesy of The Statue of Liberty—Ellis Island Foundation.

These new immigrants knew that jobs would be waiting, but they knew practically nothing about the character, culture, and traditions of America.

In the early 1900s America could best be described as a Protestant nation. The people that founded, settled, and grew it were largely from northern and western Europe and overwhelmingly Protestant. The leading politicians, educators, financiers, and businessmen in turn were Protestant. Michael Beschloss, writing in *The Conquerors*, told of a 1942 conversation between the country's Jewish secretary of the treasury, Henry Morgenthau, and a leading Catholic member of the administration, Leo Crowley. Crowley related that President Franklin Roosevelt had told him, "You know this is a Protestant country, and you Jews and Catholics are here under sufferance." This statement by Roosevelt was his assessment of the sentiment of the country, not necessarily a personal prejudice. Roosevelt had been a courageous, vocal supporter of Catholic Al Smith's quest for the Democratic presidential nomination in 1924 (lost by Smith in a rancorous contest that lent credence to FDR's conclusion).

In contrast to the original northern and western European settlers, the immigrants of the early 1900s were mainly from eastern and southern Europe, and primarily Catholic. Earlier, in the mid 1800s, when large numbers of the "Famine Irish" fled Ireland for America during the potato blight, they encountered widespread resistance and agitation from the "Know-Nothings," a group dedicated to preserving America as an outpost for Protestantism and Anglo-Saxony. (A desire to exclude these Irish was present as early as 1750, when Benjamin Franklin wrote an essay, "Observations Concerning the Increase of Mankind, Peopling of Countries etc.", in which, among other things, he attempted to convince the colonies to discourage immigration from continental Europe and Catholic Ireland, recommending instead English, Welsh, and Protestant Irish settlers.) Irish immigrants of the 1800s met resistance in society and in the workplace, with "Irish Need Not Apply" signs appearing on numerous business establishments. However, the government did not place any restrictions on their numbers.

But in the early 1900s, as immigrant numbers swelled, there were increased calls from the self-proclaimed "Native Americans" to restrict the influx of these so-called less desirable people. The "Know-Nothing" groups that had harassed the Irish were no longer in existence, but a great deal of the hate rhetoric directed toward these new immigrants came from the newly revived Ku Klux Klan. In addition to African Americans who had been targeted since after the Civil War, this new generation of the KKK railed against Catholics and Jews. They complained that big business' love of money led them to seek cheap labor by bringing in "European riff-raff", people of "inferior races"—a conclusion anyone aware of the contributions of people like Dante, Da Vinci, Galileo, Tesla, Michelangelo, Copernicus, and Marconi might find puzzling.

Native-born Americans who were less prejudicial were nonetheless fearful of the large numbers of immigrants, concerned about their jobs and the character and stability of their neighborhoods. Acting upon these feelings, the United States Congress passed a literacy test and a series of quota and national origin laws that openly discriminated against southern and eastern Europeans while favoring the Nordics. The last of these laws, passed in 1924, restricted the total number of immigrants, barred Asians entirely, and based the allowable number of immigrants from western nations upon the percentage of their population in the 1890 U.S. census. Since the majority of eastern and southern Europeans came after 1890, this law served to minimize their further immigration.

JOURNEY OF A DEPRESSION-ERA HOBO

None of this had any effect on Vincent and Stella's decision to leave Poland for America. My grandfather had no thoughts of becoming a politician, a business tycoon, or a man of influence. Questions about the dominant culture and religion of the country, about quota laws, about who were desirable or undesirable people for America he left for others to discuss. Vincent Szalanski's goals were much more modest. He wanted to earn enough money to provide a decent living for his family, and the jobs that were waiting in the mills and the mines would provide that good living. Though these goals appear modest to many, they were nonetheless formidable to Vincent. He would be in a new country, having to learn a new language and adjust to a new way of life, while almost all of the people he relied on for support would remain in Poland. There would many difficult moments ahead.

The forty-five day trip across the ocean must have allowed Vincent and Stella considerable time to think about their new life. Although the trip was long and their steerage section was not equipped for comfort, coming from living in sparse conditions, they and their three young children adapted well. The family's biggest difficulty may have happened when boarding. According to family stories, the surging crowd jostled young two-year-old Jean from her parent's grasp while walking up the gangplank, and she appeared to be headed for a fall into the sea. Quick reactions by Vincent and Stella prevented a mishap. Then, it was on to America.

As noted, the family settled in Vandergrift, Pennsylvania, where Vincent went to work for the American Sheet and Tin Plate

Company. Vandergrift was and is a town of some renown among those familiar with town planning and landscape architecture. It was designed by the landscape architecture firm of Frederick Law Olmsted, known for its work on New York City's Central Park, the grounds around the Capitol Building in Washington, D.C., and the park systems in Boston and Buffalo. This town, for which ground was broken in 1895, was the result of the vision and idealism of George C. McMurtry, who named the town in which he would build his new plant after his friend and business partner in the steel industry, Jacob J. Vandergrift.

Vandergrift Plaque
Photograph courtesy of the Victorian Vandergrift Museum and Historical Society

While planning for this expansion project, McMurtry visited industrial towns throughout the United States and Europe, looking for ideas on what to incorporate into his town and what to avoid. He found an interested partner in Olmsted, who himself had toured England in an effort to become acquainted with potential problems common in population centers that grew alongside large manufacturing complexes. Together, these men wanted their new town to be a better place for workers to live.

Individually owned houses, a system of parklets, and streets with gently rounded curves that followed the natural contour of the land helped to accomplish this. Vandergrift soon grew, largely through annexation, from its original Olmsted design, a growth necessary to accommodate the immigrants coming to work in McMurtry's mill.

By 1913, Vincent and Stella were able to buy a house on McKinley Avenue in East Vandergrift. East Vandergrift was changing in character at that time, and would soon be inhabited virtually entirely by eastern Europeans from present-day Poland, Czechoslovakia, and Lithuania. Although all were Catholic, each ethnic group established its own church, and by the early 1920s, there were three Catholic churches in East Vandergrift, along with three social clubs, each serving its particular ethnic group.

It was here that my grandparents' new life began. The ocean had been crossed and Poland gone from their lives, save in memory. Western Pennsylvania was one of the world's foremost steel-making centers and Poles had been coming to its mills for decades—so much so, that by March 1907, 11,697 of the 14,359 common laborers in Carnegie-owned plants in Allegheny County were eastern European. These new immigrants were assigned the most difficult and dangerous jobs, and as one laborer wrote in a letter home:

> *There are different kinds of work, heavy and light, but a man from our country cannot get the light. Wherever the heat is most insupportable, the flames most scorching, the smoke and soot most choking, there we are certain to find compatriots spent and wasted with toil!*
>
> (Source: Brody, *Steelworkers in America*)

Too often, the workers were treated as merely means of production, not unlike machines or raw materials. Accidents and fatalities were considered part of the workday and factored into the cost of expenses. From 1906 to 1910 almost one fourth of the recent immigrants working in the South Works in Pittsburgh (3,273 men) suffered an accident, and in one year alone, 127 men from eastern Europe were killed in Allegheny County's steel mills. The dead left not only huge emotional voids that would never be filled, but also long term financial problems for their surviving families.

Many of the eastern and southern European men who came to work in the steel mills during the late 1890s or very early 1900s came alone with intentions of working hard, saving some money and returning home. Entry-level wages were so meager that it was too difficult to support a wife and children, and the loneliness, low wages, dangerous work, and loss of jobs during low production periods sent hundreds of thousands of eastern and southern Europeans back to Europe (an estimated 590,000 returned from

1908-1910). Nevertheless, more arrived and by 1920 there were more than four million Italians and more than two million Poles in America.

When my grandfather, Vincent Szalanski, went into the Vandergrift mill in 1910, wages had risen to where they could now support families. His family grew, with Matthew born in 1911, Stanley in 1913, Laura in 1914, and twins Sophia and Zigmund in 1917. Vincent's experience as a blacksmith in Poland enabled him to escape the more difficult, dangerous, and lower paying jobs usually reserved for immigrants. The blacksmith department, part of maintenance, made, maintained, and repaired plant equipment. This involved heavy physical exertion and sustained exposure to heat, as the material had to be heated to the correct forging temperature. Even so, it was one of the safer departments.

Blacksmith Department of Vandergrift Mill – 1913.
Photograph courtesy of the Victorian Vandergrift Museum and Historical Society.

Men who worked in the blast furnace, open-hearth, and re-heat furnace areas were exposed to severely extreme heat, in excess of 2000 degrees. Their danger was such that a job description for an open-hearth worker included the admonition "failure could result in total disability or death." These steelworkers of the late nineteenth and early twentieth centuries performed some of the most physically difficult tasks ever demanded in the pursuit of legitimate commerce. And they did it for long, long hours. Until the 1920s, they worked twelve hour shifts, seven days a week, a schedule that prompted a Carnegie Company official, W. R. Jones, to declare back in 1881, "it was entirely out of the question to expect human flesh and blood to labor incessantly for twelve hours." Nonetheless, this brutal workweek persisted for another forty years. A strike initiated by western Pennsylvania steelworkers in 1919 eventually led to an eight hour work day and shorter work weeks, enabling the workers to create lives beyond that of beasts of burden.

CHAPTER 3
AMERICA IN THE 1920s

The surge of manufacturing in this decade set America on its way to becoming the World's most wealthy and powerful nation.

Photograph courtesy of the Rivers of Steel National Heritage Area.

This period when steelworkers were afforded some relief and dignity was a time of major change in America. The 1920s, widely referred to as the Roaring Twenties, were beginning, arriving on the heels of World War I and the great influenza epidemic, which in 1918 and 1919 killed twice the amount of people that died in the war (a half million Americans and twenty-one million worldwide succumbed to the disease).

The Allied victory in the war brought a welcomed corollary occurrence for the Szalanskis—the reemergence of Poland as a sovereign nation—but the epidemic brought tragedy to the DeMicheles with the loss of Domenick's brother, Pietro, one of a surprisingly large number of seemingly healthy young adults victimized by the flu outbreak.

As the 1920s dawned, an atmosphere conducive for optimism was building. The United States had emerged from World War I as a world power, both politically and industrially, with its economy soon to account for nearly half the world's manufacturing.

Two constitutional amendments were ratified in the years ushering in this decade, one that permanently changed politics in America, and the other, repealed in 1933, that gave a distinctive aura to the 1920s. The latter, the Eighteenth Amendment, ratified in 1919, became know as Prohibition, as it prohibited the manufacture, sale, or transport of alcoholic beverages. This amendment became another factor in the cultural divide between the native born, typically Protestant, rural Americans, and urban, often Catholic, Americans. Rural voters supported it; urban voters opposed it. Prohibition's adoption had the unintended effect of creating an illegal liquor trade, largely controlled by gangsters, and the emergence of more than thirty thousand "speakeasies", where the public went for entertainment and to illegally consume alcohol.

The Nineteenth Amendment was ratified in 1920, granting universal suffrage to women, and has had an obvious influence in every local, state, and national election since.

The Roaring Twenties were ultimately defined by economic success and the optimism it generated. Industrial output nearly doubled from 1920 to 1929, with new products spewing forth and new companies formed to produce them. Jobs were so plentiful and labor so scarce that some businesses pressed state legislatures to pass compulsory work laws. The Ku Klux Klan even distributed leaflets proclaiming, "No man has a right to consume without producing." People began to believe that the country had reached a permanent plateau of prosperity, and this high level of optimism persisted through the decade to such an extent that President Herbert Hoover, in his inaugural address of March, 1929, said, "In no nation are the fruits of accomplishment more secure."

The social pattern of the country was also changing. At the turn of the century, America was a mostly rural, agricultural society. The 1900 census showed only forty percent of its population living in urban settings, with "urban" classified as any city, town, and a village with 2,500 or more inhabitants. This number rose to a majority of fifty-one percent by 1920, reflecting the massive influx of immigrants who settled in urban areas for jobs and the great migration of African Americans from the rural south to higher paying jobs in the industrial north. This changing character of America continued throughout the decade to such a degree that the 1930 census recorded fifty-six percent of its citizens living in urban areas.

This massive immigration also affected the character of the country in another way. The predominantly Catholic immigrants increased the minority Catholic population enough to weaken the total dominance exercised by Protestants. The growing strength of this community helped the Democrats nominate Catholic Alfred Smith as their presidential candidate in 1928, the first time a major political party in the United States chose a member of that religion to run for the nation's highest office.

Such was the decade in which my father, Joe Szalanski, came of age and grew into adulthood. East Vandergrift in this era was an especially good place for a kid to grow up. Lying at the foot of a large hillside, sandwiched between the hill and Kiskiminetas River, with a steep road the only way in and out, it was physically isolated from the town of Vandergrift, and somewhat socially isolated as well. Inhabited virtually one hundred percent by eastern Europeans, it provided new immigrants with a comforting, nurturing environment in which to begin their resolute efforts towards becoming Americans.

Although minor squabbling occasionally surfaced among the Poles, Slovaks, and Lithuanians, they all came from similar backgrounds and shared the same hopes and ambitions. Many of the immigrants had large families, so there were always plenty of kids to play with. The Szalanski family itself had eight children, the

DeMicheles would also grow to eight, with Julia, Albert, Ann and Adele joining John, Nick, Joe and Louise.

The Szalanski family. Joe immediately to his father's right.

The DeMichele family - 1918. Albert, Ann, and Adele were born after this picture was taken, and there never was a full family portrait with all eight children. Louise is to her mother's left.

BOARDING THE WESTBOUND

Vincent Szalanski took advantage of the four-hour reduction in the daily mill shifts and the shorter workweek at the mill to open a blacksmith shop on the property behind his house. His new side business did well and Joe, as the oldest son, helped him in the shop. Learning the value of work at an early age is undeniably beneficial and usually serves one well throughout life. However, Joe also had ample time for carefree play. One of his passions was baseball, and there were two ball fields and plenty of children in East Vandergrift. Unlike today, adults were not heavily involved in organizing the youngsters, so Joe and his friends formed their own teams, scheduled the games, made and enforced the rules. They played ball, had fun together and gave each other nicknames—Beppo, Pipe, Dodge, Kelly, Joker, Hammer, and Flunky. Flunky was Joe. Later, Joe's devotion to baseball showed up in his hobo journal, where he wrote of the effort he made to listen to some of the 1932 World Series:

> *Got a freight to Montevideo, Minn. a little too late to listen to the ball game, but on the next day, ...got my dinner with ease, made it my business not to miss the 2nd game of the World Series. I went to town all washed up, sat in front of a radio store and was in on the big game.*

My father's talents in the game didn't rise to the level of his passion for it. The best players had names like Dodge and Beppo, the latter's strong arm making him a local legend. Once, when pitching for a local team against a professional minor league team from the area, the minor leaguers' manager asked that Beppo be removed from the mound because he was showing-up the professionals. Beppo and his friend, Leo, were also part of a fundraising scheme. They would drive to a nearby town, then Leo would point out an object seemingly out of range of a thrown baseball, and take bets that somebody could do it. Once the locals bit, Beppo threw, Leo collected and they went on to another town.

Like Joe, Beppo later hopped freights while unemployed in the Depression and Joe noted in his diary that he and Kelly met Beppo and Pipe in Bridgeport, Connecticut in August 1932. Unlike Joe, Beppo was actually looking for work and he and Pipe went only as far as the New England states. Unfortunately, family circumstances forced Beppo into the mill and away from professional baseball.

(Years later, in the 1950s, a son of one of Vandergrift's eastern European immigrants would pitch in the major leagues. North Vandergrift's Rudy Minarcin became a hard-throwing pitcher for the Cincinnati Reds and Boston Red Sox, a man who pitched a one-hitter for Cincinnati against the Pirates in Pittsburgh—a game attended by a large group of admiring fans from Vandergrift.)

While East Vandergrift provided a solid base and support, these children of eastern European immigrants needed a larger sphere of influence if they were to become Americans. The public school system was an integral part of this process. The kids from East Vandergrift met children from every other part of town, from every ethnic group, every race, and every religion. They took the same classes, played the same games, participated in the same activities. They would come to like some of the new kids, dislike some, and discover there were more similarities than differences among the varied groups of people.

Still, in Vandergrift, as in most industrial towns, there was limited social interaction among the various components of society, especially for members of Vincent's generation. Each ethnic group formed its own social clubs, retreats where they could reminisce about the Old World and keep alive its treasured traditions. The proliferation of these ethnic clubs was also due in part by the reluctance and outright refusal of many native born to welcome the newcomers into their lodges and clubs. With the immigrants clustered in separate sections of town, there was scant social interaction between them and the native born in the neighborhoods. And because the new immigrants were almost all Catholic and the earlier residents Protestant, they didn't see each other at church, either. Thus, the only sustained contact among the adults occurred in the workplace. In the mill where Vincent worked, men of all nationalities, religions and races relied on each other for personal safety and to maintain production at levels satisfactory enough to ensure job security. Of course, this didn't immediately lead to the various groups inviting each other into their homes and lodges, and immigrants continued to face hostility for their strange ways, strange names, and strange languages. Assimilation took time, but all parties began to gradually respect the others.

Because of his trade, Vincent's work in the mill was not as harsh as that of most immigrants. Being a blacksmith also earned him higher wages, and this, combined with the income from his shop, led him to become one of the wealthier men in East Vandergrift. He was the first person there to own an automobile. For years after Henry Ford completed his first Model T, the automobile was a luxury item. However, mass production eventually lowered the cost and by 1920 there were eight million in use, a number that tripled during the opulent years of the 1920s. Popular usage of the automobile led to the building of the country's vast highway network, cutting travel time and granting access to places heretofore inaccessible.

Other new products taking hold in the 1920s also impacted lifestyles far into the future. After having been employed in action in World War I, the airplane was beginning to come more widely into use in this decade. It was not generally used by the public in that decade, remaining in developmental and experimental stages, and the domain of daredevils and adventurers. Its impact on the future of America and the world was probably beyond the imaginations of most people in that era.

In Pittsburgh, in 1920, radio station KDKA created the first radio broadcast. Now people could buy a product that brought strangers' voices into their houses. They could be informed and entertained, and since the informers and entertainers did so in English, immigrants were aided in learning the new language. This new phenomenon quickly spread through the country. There were twenty-eight radio stations at the beginning of 1922 and nearly six hundred by the end, with hundreds of companies formed to manufacture radio sets. These sets, rapidly purchased by an eager public, brought a stream of new personalities and programs into homes. This was significant in the following decade, when excitement coming from radios provided some relief from the worry caused by the Great Depression. Social workers of that era reported destitute families that chose to give up furniture and iceboxes before they would part with their radios. As my father recalled in his diary, people at one of his stops had not parted with their radios (and sadly for him, would not easily part with their food):

> *I got to Barstow, CA at 7 o'clock in the morning, went to 15 houses for breakfast, the radios would be playing, as soon as I knocked on the door the radio got turned off and nobody home!*

Entertainment also came from motion pictures. The 1920s saw an explosive growth of this industry, and by the middle of the decade there were some twenty thousand theaters throughout the country showing silent films. The first talking film, *The Jazz Singer*, was released in 1927. These new forms of entertainment and transportation were joined by the introduction of new labor saving electrical appliances, including toasters, irons, vacuum cleaners, stoves, and refrigerators.

For most Americans, these innovations reinforced their belief in the omnipotence of business. There was a constant stream of new products, easy credit to help purchase them, and a rising stock market in which more and more people were investing. It was a heady time, and overwhelming for many of the new immigrants. Some Italians would greet each other with the phrase, *America ay futa per tay*, meaning, "America was made for you!" It was an inside joke, affirming they were fortunate to be here, and acknowledging that they wouldn't be living this well back in Italy.

My maternal grandfather, Domenick DeMichele, was one of the Italians seeing more money, and he was earning it. He crawled through a tunnel into a coal mine every day, walking three miles to get there and three miles back when the day's work was done. The mine's ceiling was so low that the men were unable to stand, and the miners spent the entire day on their knees digging coal from the ground. Domenick endured this difficult way of making a living, but tried to guide his sons away from the mines. His next-door neighbor, Ernie, had a shoe repair shop and Domenick's eldest son, John, went to work for Ernie on a part-time basis at age sixteen, and then continued to work and learn the trade. A few doors away, Felix, another neighbor, operated a barbershop, and Domenick's son, Joe, was sent to observe in hopes he would later learn to be a barber. Nick was the first to graduate from high school and kept his grades at or near the top of his class. While still in high school, Nick worked at American Sheet and Tin Plate on Saturdays. After graduating in June 1929, he planned to work one year in the mill, save the money, and attend college the following year.

John, the eldest, left school to work full time in the shoe shop. Ernie treated him as an apprentice, taught him the craft and provided a small wage. His siblings fondly remember their kindhearted brother spending his money on treats for them—ice cream, candy, trips to the movies. John became an accomplished shoemaker and eventually bought a shop in Morgantown, West Virginia in the late 1930s. Several generations of Morgantown residents brought shoes to his Met Shoe Shop on High Street, a site that became a local landmark. John was never one to focus on making money, and his prices and credit terms were known to be more than generous. He did set one business goal for himself, however, one that he failed to achieve. John planned to operate his sole-proprietorship until he was ninety years old, but couldn't do it. He had to close shortly after his eighty-ninth birthday when his arthritis worsened. Still, he gave his customers excellent service until then.

The plan to escape the mills worked for my uncle, John, but life's unplanned and unforeseen circumstances sidetracked Nick and Joe. Both spent their working lives in the steel mill, doing well and raising good families, and both were with my father at the Irvin Works on that tragic day in March 1940.

By the latter years of the 1920s, the older Szalanski children were also growing up and moving out. Marta and Jean left home to work as live-in housekeepers. This was common practice among Polish girls of this era, who often moved great distances. Marta went to Buffalo and Jean to Newark, and each married in their new location, with Jean remaining in Newark for life and Marta moving to California. My father, Joe, briefly moved to Chicago after his eighteenth birthday, a favored destination for young Polish-American men. His uncle, Joseph Klonowski, lived there with the intention of saving some money and returning to the native country, which he did.

JOURNEY OF A DEPRESSION-ERA HOBO

Uncle Joseph and Aunt Salome Klonowski after Uncle Joe returned to Poland.

Chicago was the nation's second largest city, and housed large Catholic, foreign-born, and Polish populations. When my father lived there, he had the comfort and familiarity of living among fellow eastern Europeans, along with the adventure and excitement of living in one of the world's great cities. He obtained a job in a radio sales and service store in a Polish section of the city, keeping him away from hard physical labor and in touch with a growth industry. The growth of this and all other industries seemed to have no limit, as our business and political leaders regularly reiterated an unquestioned faith in the economy. Prohibition, and the characters that surrounded it, are closely identified with the era, but the booming economy really defined it. Presidents Harding and Coolidge followed the practice of minimal government interference with business, and newspapers wrote of the government being completely fused with business.

Optimism, validated by nearly a decade of dazzling success, was contagious. Low-level immigrant laborers felt secure in their jobs and saw opportunity for their children; business owners and executives saw unlimited potential with expanding profits, salaries, and stock market returns. This was one of those times in history when people thought they had it figured out. More products were introduced, more companies formed, more profits made, more jobs created, and more record highs were recorded for the stock market.

Everyone watched as stock prices went up, up again, and up even further. More and more people bought stocks, often with borrowed money. Not everybody could afford to purchase stocks, but about one million Americans became involved in this method of making easy money through investing, or speculating. Times were good.

The presidential election of 1928 came in the midst of those good times. Catholic Al Smith, as the Democratic candidate, ran against Republican Herbert Hoover. It was a bitter campaign. Cynic H. L. Mencken quipped that Smith, who sought to repeal Prohibition, lost because "those who fear the Pope outnumber those who are tired of the Anti-Saloon League." Smith's religion undoubtedly was a factor in his defeat, but the country had prospered during the administrations of Republicans Harding and Coolidge, and it's historically tough for any candidate to run against peace and prosperity.

JOURNEY OF A DEPRESSION-ERA HOBO

When President Hoover said, "in no nation are the fruits of accomplishment more secure," he reaffirmed the notion of a permanent plateau of prosperity, and few doubted him. But few also realized that the stock market boom would continue only as long as new money came into it, either through new speculators or by the commitment of additional funds by those already invested.

On a personal level, tragedy struck the DeMichele family several weeks after Hoover's optimistic inaugural speech. On April 22, 1929, Domenick DeMichele suffered a fatal stroke. All the prosperity in the country meant nothing; there was only grief and sorrow for the passing of this kind, courageous man, a good husband, a good father. In some circles, my grandfather, Domenick, was one of countless, indistinguishable laborers of his era. But just like the wealthy and famous, these men, too, had aspirations and talents. My grandfather's greatest talents were botanical. His sizable backyard had space devoted to a vegetable garden, fruit trees, and grapevines. But his flowers—lilacs, irises, and a rose-covered trellis, graced much of the rest. Far from the harsh demands of the coal mines, these flowers, and his family, were his passions. After his untimely death, my grandmother, Angeline, and the children had to take care of one other. John and Louise had already left school to help financially. Now, Nick's college plans ended, as well as Joe's barbershop, replaced by working in the mill. Julia, Albert, and Ann were still in school, and Adele, only four, had yet to start. Life for the DeMicheles would change.

Chapter 4
HARD TIMES

The Great Depression

As the country sunk into a Depression foreclosures and evictions soared, forcing people from their homes. Here, a homeless man living in his car is given a meal from the Salvation Army.

Photograph of The Salvation Army National Archives

Six months later, life throughout America changed. Full employment gave way to shuttered factories, closed businesses and massive unemployment; prosperity was replaced with poverty; optimism turned to fear. The day had come when people finally became unable or unwilling to put more money into buying stocks, and a virtual absence of buyers sent stock prices inexorably downward. Selling momentum grew to such a panic that investors dumped their holdings for any price. By the time the market closed on October 29, 1929, stocks had lost ten billion dollars in value. This day is widely associated with the beginning of the Great Depression. There are those who will argue that it was not the actual beginning but prominent economist John Kenneth Galbraith assigns significant responsibility to the Crash. He wrote, "any satisfactory explanation of the Autumn of 1929 and thereafter must accord a dignified role to the speculative boom and ensuing collapse. Until September or October 1929, the decline in economic activity was very modest." Others subscribed to the view that the market slump was merely a reflection of a declining industrial situation. But there is no doubt about the effect "Black Tuesday" had on peoples' finances and psyches. The great economic boom of the '20s seemed to have exploded on the floor of the New York Stock Exchange, very definitively, very emphatically.

History can record the date, the precise number of percentage points the Dow Jones Average fell, and the exact magnitude of price drops of individual stocks. What it cannot precisely convey is the shock and fear felt by individual investors. These were people who were wealthy only days ago, now thrown into sudden poverty.

Investors, many of who had never seen a significant decline in stock prices, stood by helplessly as their stocks became practically worthless.

When the collapse came, it fell not only on speculators looking for quick riches, but on working Americans making long term investments, and on widows and the elderly relying on income from the market. There was no way to recoup the losses. The stock market remained at its new diminished level and unemployment soared to unprecedented highs. With no availability of investment capital, companies reduced production and many failed altogether, putting millions out of work. By 1932, American industry was turning out less than half its 1929 value, and soon a full one-fourth of all heads of households were unemployed.

The downward spiral was hastened by problems in the banking industry, as bank failures heaped additional doom and suffering onto an already gloomy situation. By 1933 there were eleven thousand fewer banks than in 1929; 'The Citizen Bank of Vandergrift among those that closed. The monetary collapse was so gigantic that between 1929 and 1933 there was a full one-third reduction in the deposits of currency held by the public.

Economists looked for reasons for the meltdown, examining what propelled the great economic expansion of the 1920s, then tried to determine what caused the demise of it all. This subject is so complex that decades after it happened, Galbraith wrote that "the causes of the Great Depression are still uncertain" and the current chair of the Federal Reserve Bank, Bernard Bernake, took it a step further, writing, "to understand the Great Depression is the Holy Grail of Maco-economists." However, at the time, many put forth simpler answers. Typical of this was former Louisiana Governor Huey Long who put the blame directly on "the grinning devils of Wall Street."

While the precise causes of the Depression were of great interest to economists and politicians, they didn't really matter much to the general public. They were too busy trying to deal with its effects.

As the Depression took hold, the spirit of the country changed beyond recognition. The mayor of Detroit testified to a senate subcommittee that the "city's relief rolls embraced doctors, lawyers, ministers, and two families after whom streets are named." In Stud Terkel's *Hard Times— An Oral History of the Great Depression*, he quotes a Chicagoan:

> *We lost everything. I sold the car for $15 in order to buy some food for the family. I would bend my head low in the relief line so nobody would recognize me.*

These lines became a way of life, and people became less embarrassed because so many were doing it.

Hundreds of thousands of Americans defaulted on their mortgages and rent payments and were forced to find alternative shelter. They moved into caves, sewer pipes, and abandoned boxcars. Known as Hoovervilles, homeless camps and shantytowns with living quarters made of corrugated iron, wood, and packing crates, grew around most large cities. Those who slept outdoors covered themselves with newspapers referred to as "Hoover Blankets."

A "Hooverville" in Oregon.
Photograph courtesy of The Library of Congress.

New York City attributed 190 deaths in 1934 to starvation and cited large increases in malnutrition and dysentery. In Detroit, the vice chairman of the city's unemployment commission saw "no possibility of preventing widespread hunger and slow starvation." This didn't happen, but the threat of starvation was real and wore down the spirits of the unemployed.

In the early 1930s, there was no unemployment compensation and no organized welfare system. Local governments did have some relief agencies, but they were not equipped to handle a crisis of this magnitude. In the spring of 1932, New York City had twenty-five thousand cases on its emergency list waiting for relief.

BOARDING THE WESTBOUND

In this era, government was not expected to provide more than minimal support for the unemployed or any other group in need. The accepted notion was that families would care for themselves, especially their children and elderly. This notion saw the Szalanskis and DeMicheles through the Depression.

The DeMicheles had the more difficult time because of Domenick's death shortly before the Depression. John, Nick, and my mother, Louise, all lived at home and used their incomes to help Angeline cover the household expenses. Domenick's brother, Tomaso, who immigrated in 1923, also lived in the house and contributed his coal miner's wages and there was some aide from the county and the local Salvation Army. The family maintained a backyard vegetable garden and fruit trees, and the younger children helped with household chores and contributed financially as they grew older.

These efforts were supplemented by assistance from two of the children's godfathers. Coomba (Godfather) Luigi, who lived near Harrisburg and worked steadily throughout the Depression for the Pennsylvania Railroad, took his role as godfather seriously. He sent a money order to the family every month and several times a year would use his employee's rail pass to escort a turkey to Vandergrift for a family dinner. Coomba Nunzio, who operated a chicken farm a few miles from Vandergrift, provided chickens and eggs for family meals. This help was significant, for as the Depression deepened, Tomaso lost his job in the mines and work was rationed at the mill to the point where Nick's paycheck of February 28, 1933 was for $.01 (one penny).

JOURNEY OF A DEPRESSION-ERA HOBO

A paycheck received by Nick DeMichele on February 28, 1933.
Photograph courtesy of Angie Loperfito.

The financial situation would have improved had Angeline accepted any one of the offers she received in 1930 to become a "bootlegger" and sell illegal liquor from the house. A widow with eight kids was seen as a good cover for an illegal distributor, but Angeline declined. Her family survived the Depression with each other's help, and while money saved from bootlegging might have prevented the sheriff's sale of 1940, neither Angeline nor any of the children ever doubted the wisdom of her decision.

The Szalanski family fared reasonably well during these tough times. Vandergrift's American Sheet and Tin Plate Plant was able to keep its employees working until early 1932 with backlogged orders, and when production was cut and work schedules reduced, Vincent's maintenance department continued to work more than most. Like most families, they had a vegetable garden in the backyard and Marta and Jean sent a little money home from Buffalo and Newark. Chicago was hit hard by the Depression. By 1932, 750,000 Chicagoans were unemployed, and of the 228 banks there in 1929, only fifty-one were still open. My father, Joe, lost his job and returned to the family home in East Vandergrift. The Szalanski home, about fifty yards from the railroad tracks, was filled with sounds of trains riding by, trains imagined to be heading to far off places. The promise of new places grew more alluring during the Depression, when massive unemployment threw millions into idleness. Thousands began riding freight cars and drifting from town to town. Some went looking for work; some went for adventure. Many felt a sense of failure, and simply abandoned the families they could no longer support. They crowded the trains, so much so that Joe wrote from Amarillo, Texas:

> *First one on the boxcar, about the time it was ready to go, about 35 men and 2 women. Well, I was lucky to have a place to spread my blanket. Lots stand up all night cause there was no place to lay.*

Chapter 5
HOBO CULTURE

Hobos would walk the tracks to the next place where a train would stop or slow down enough to be boarded.

Photograph courtesy of The Library of Congress.

"Hobo's Lullaby" is a song written by George Reeves, and famously performed by various people including folk singer Woody Guthrie, his son Arlo Guthrie, Pete Seeger, Emmylou Harris, the Kingston Trio, and Ramblin' Jack Elliott. Its music is based on the Carter Family song "Thinking tonight of my blue eyes," which in turn derives its melodic structure from popular Civil War era composer George F. Root's song "Just before the Battle, Mother". Hobos Lullaby by George Reeves © Copyright 1961 (renewed) by Sanga Music, Inc.

Go to sleep you weary hobo
Let the towns drift slowly by
Can't you hear the steel rails hummin'
That's the hobo's lullaby

I know your clothes are torn and ragged
And your hair is turning gray
Lift your head and smile at trouble
You'll find peace and rest someday

Now don't you worry 'bout tomorrow
Let tomorrow come and go
Tonight you're in a nice warm boxcar
Safe from all that wind and snow

I know the police cause you trouble
They cause trouble everywhere
But when you die and go to Heaven
You'll find no policemen there

JOURNEY OF A DEPRESSION-ERA HOBO

So go to sleep you weary hobo
Let the towns drift slowly by
Listen to the steel rails hummin'
That's a hobo's lullaby

Lyrics courtesy of Sanga Music, Inc. New York, NY

The Depression-spawned transients were newcomers to riding the rails—a way of life that had existed for more than a half century. Since the expansion of railroads, from nine thousand miles of track in the United States in 1850 to more than two hundred fifty thousand miles in 1913, there had been people who built their lives around traveling on freight cars. Having no permanent residences or employment, they survived by working temporary and short-term jobs as they roamed, and since they had nowhere in particular to be, they roamed wherever they pleased. This freedom of being able to follow any tracks they chose, to ride to any destination they fancied, had helped them become part of American folklore, referred to by some as, "Knights of the Road." They formed a loose confederation, bound together primarily through allegiance and adherence to their novel way of life, guided by their precept of "don't own anything you have to feed or paint", living by a voluntary, self-policed code. Their Hobo Code, displayed at the Convention Congress of the Hobos of America held in Chicago in August 1894, encompassed the following tenets:

BOARDING THE WESTBOUND

Decide your own life, don't let another person run or rule you.

When in town, always respect the local law and officials, and try to be a gentleman at all times.

Don't take advantage of someone else who is in a vulnerable situation, locals, or other hobos.

Always try to find work, even if temporary, and always seek out jobs nobody wants. By doing so you not only help a business along, but insure employment should you return to that town again.

When no employment is available, make your own work by using your added talents at crafts.

Do not allow yourself to become a stupid drunk and set a bad example for local's treatment of other hobos.

When jungling in town, respect handouts, do not wear them out, another hobo will be coming along who will need them as bad, if not worse than you.

Always respect nature, do not leave garbage where you are jungling.

If in a community jungle, always pitch in and help. Try to stay clean, and boil up whenever possible.

JOURNEY OF A DEPRESSION-ERA HOBO

When traveling, ride trains respectfully, take no personal chances, cause no problems with the operating crew or host railroad, and act like an extra crewmember.

Do not cause problems in a train yard. Another hobo will be coming along who will need passage through that yard.

Do not allow other hobos to molest children, expose to authorities all molesters, they are the worst garbage to infest any society.

Help all runaway children, and try to induce them to return home.

Help your fellow hobos whenever and wherever needed, you may need their help someday.

If present at a hobo court and you have testimony, give it whether for or against the accused, your voice counts.

The people who live by this code are part of a unique, somewhat endearing sub-culture. In contrast to mainstream society where people may be measured by the size of their house, make of car, and prestige of their career, hobos have no house, no car, and no career. Whereas high achievers trumpet 24/7 availability, hobos are available only when they choose to be. The

BOARDING THE WESTBOUND

Britt (IA) News Tribune quotes a present day hobo regarding this lifestyle:

> ...imagine a way of life where you are not bound by time schedules, home owner bills, job expectations, the IRS, you can live where you want as long as its in the Continental U.S. and Canada. Never pay a travel fare unless you want to, never pay rent, electric, gas, water, or cable bills, never pay taxes, and see places in the U. S. and Canada others only see in the movies or in a magazine.

They feel a grand sense of camaraderie among themselves, a feeling that extends beyond when their earthly rides are over. At the Hobo Cemetery in Britt, Iowa, the deceased are fondly remembered with prayers, poetry, and music during Britt's annual hobo convention. Headstones of hobos laid to rest carry colorful names like Slow Motion Shorty, Fishbones, Cinder Box Cindy, Connecticut Slim, and the Hard Rock Kid. They are respectfully referred to as "friends who caught the westbound," echoing a phrase commonly used by railroaders when recalling departed colleagues.

JOURNEY OF A DEPRESSION-ERA HOBO

Hobo cemetery in Britt. Final resting place for some "friends who caught the westbound."
Photograph courtesy of the Hobo Foundation in Britt, IA.

Although their nicknames lent a special aura to the hobo way of life, there was a darker side, beginning with the physical perils of hopping on and off the trains. The Hobo Code exhorts travelers to "ride trains respectfully, take no personal chances." They were cautioned to be careful on what hobos called the "rolling giants," instructed to board trains only when they were going between five and ten miles per hour. New riders were warned of the dangers and reminded that many train derailments resulted from irresponsible hobo behavior. During the Depression, unfortunately, there were thousands of inexperienced newcomers, all of whom were susceptible to serious injury. After passing Redding, California, my father recorded:

BOARDING THE WESTBOUND

> *Indian fellow tried to hop on the freight I was on, he missed the step and got his leg cut off. I saw him after he pulled his self away from the cars, freight never stopped. Next division I was to go uptown, grab some grub. Brakeman asks me if I had seen the fellow get his leg cut off, I said yes, I saw him after it was cut off. Calls me into the yard office, have your breakfast yet, I said no, he brought me hot cakes and two cups coffee. I told him I saw it after it was cut off, that's all there is to it. Plenty of other guys saw it but I was the only one to get anything out of it.*

Once safely aboard, hobos were constantly exposed to the elements—extreme cold, extreme heat, driving rains, almost always without proper protective clothing. People across all segments of society struggled for adequate clothing in the Depression, and hobos were among the least likely to have what they needed. Joe endured this exposure to the elements, and was bothered in various regions of the country in different times of the year. He wrote:

> *Only 12 houses in this town of Thalmann, Georgia and talk about mosquitoes biting, my arms, neck and back are just full of mosquito bites, and the drinking water is terrible, tastes like rotten eggs. People around here say it is the most healthful water in the world, but if you ask me it is rotten. The weather is so darn hot*

that you can burn up in 1 hour under the sun. Sweat is rolling off all parts of your body just as though it were raining. I had to take off all my clothes except my pants and shoes, and my pants are very wet right now. At the present time, I have more mosquito bites than a pickle has warts.

Later, in Trinidad, Colorado, he noted:

I went to a house and asked for coffee. I told the lady I wanted to take it along with me and boil it in the jungle, she said I could eat in her house. The lady told me the reason she made me eat in her house. She said a young fellow about my age froze to death one winter near the water tank, and she wanted to see me get away safe.

He did remain safe, but couldn't avoid the cold, as later entries describe the temperature causing him to "walk like a paralyzed man" and "shake like a leaf."

The hobo lifestyle also made access to adequate health care difficult, and Depression hobos faced imminent threats of malnutrition and exposure. Incidents of pneumonia and tuberculosis were not uncommon and local hospitals usually were severely taxed. Violence, though rare, was a threat, as ill-protected hobos were potentially easy targets for attackers. In Amarillo, Texas, Joe wrote:

BOARDING THE WESTBOUND

Two men said a couple of doped up guys were going to stick up the whole gang, everybody got stones and clubs, all set for the holdup. But it never came.

In addition to physical danger, there was physical discomfort from riding dirty boxcars, enduring periods of time without proper washing or bathing, few shaves, few haircuts, dirty clothes, and poor hygiene in general. Freights in the Depression era still absorbed discharge from coal-fueled engines. At times, the riders were so numerous that lying down to rest on the boxcar's floor was impossible.

One of the smoke-spewing engines of the era.
Photograph courtesy of The Carnegie Library of Pittsburgh.

JOURNEY OF A DEPRESSION-ERA HOBO

There was emotional discomfort, too, brought about by separation from family, and a sharp sense of vulnerability uniquely felt by those who have no money. Then there was the law. On and around the trains, railroad employees referred to as bulls sought to prevent hobos from boarding freight and ejected them when caught on board. Part of being a hobo was avoiding the bulls, both in the freight yards and aboard freights, and interaction between hobos and bulls was an interesting hide and seek game. There were states in which living as a hobo was a criminal offense, but these laws were rarely enforced during the Depression. When enforced, however, it could be done harshly. A *New York Times* article of January 15, 1933, reported that a fourteen-year old runaway charged with "hoboing" alleged being tortured on a chain gang in a South Carolina prison.

Joe obviously wasn't deterred by any thoughts of the potential discomfort or peril that riding the rails might entail. As a twenty-two year old, he was more likely focused on the perceived glamour of this lifestyle, of going where he wanted to, of seeing places he had only heard or read about. Living a block from the railroad tracks could have made him more susceptible to this, constantly hearing the mournful train whistle disappear into the distance, listening to the clacking of the rails as the trains sped to faraway places. These reflections, along with the attraction of the Hobo Code's doctrine to "Decide your own life, don't let another person run or rule you," could be a powerful temptation, a temptation that many entertain but very few ever yield to.

Chapter 6
JOE BECOMES A HOBO

Joe set out to see America, leaving the comfort and security of home for the uncertainties and excitement of life on the road.

Photograph courtesy of The Library of Congress.

Joe did. He had been, and would again become, a producer, making steel in the steel capital of the world and performing difficult and dangerous tasks in the process. But July 1932 offered a chance to step away, an opportunity to live the free life of a hobo, an opportunity to journey to all forty-eight states of the continental United States. (In 1932, this was the entire country—Alaska and Hawaii became states in 1959).

My father's trip began immediately after a dark day in our history, a day on which the U.S. Army fired upon its own World War I veterans. These veterans, demanding receipt of promised military bonuses, had camped out in Washington, D.C. and pledged to remain until Congress authorized an immediate distribution of the bonuses. When police tried to evict them from the shanties and abandoned buildings, hostilities erupted and two ex-soldiers were killed. Troops were called out that evening and descended upon the former soldiers with tanks, machine guns, and tear gas, routing them from the encampments.

Joe and his friend, Kelly, left the next day. Kelly's real name was John—his nickname was given to him because of his constant singing of Irish songs, causing his friends to conclude that he probably wasn't Polish, but Irish, and needed an Irish name. A block from Joe's house, the two hopped a Pennsylvania Railroad freight bound for Pittsburgh, changed there and went east through Altoona and Harrisburg, then north to Elmira, New York.

They were out of Pennsylvania, and the trip was on. Kelly, twenty-five, was a good storyteller and singer, and liked a good time. The reason for their trip was to have fun and an adventure.

JOURNEY OF A DEPRESSION-ERA HOBO

They weren't looking for jobs, except for short, temporary work that could get them some money or food. They weren't deserting their families, either, as they were single, planned to return home when the adventure was over, and kept in touch with the home folks through the mail.

This was the right time to be doing this. There was little fun in East Vandergrift, with unemployment and worry creating a sullen environment. Jobs and family would come later, making an adventure of this magnitude virtually impossible. This was Joe's chance to experience the feeling of freedom, and give in to the pull of the open road. The opportunity appeared, and Joe didn't hesitate.

My father lived this hobo life for a little over four months in 1932, leaving East Vandergrift on July 31 and returning December 5. He recorded his daily activities, telling where he went, how and what he ate, where he slept, and of interesting people he met and unusual events that occurred. Many of his days were unspectacular and routine; others were extraordinary. Joe slept in boxcars and under the stars, in missions and jails (fourteen times as a welcome guest of local authorities and twice under judge's orders). He bummed his food daily from private homes, restaurants, shops, and missions. In a letter he sent home from New Orleans, he wrote, "You may be thinking I'm traveling slow. Well this is the way I like to travel, you see it gives me time to look over the towns and cities." He would have written more, noting:

BOARDING THE WESTBOUND

Dear Pals: I wanted to write you a letter some time ago but paper is very scarce. I would buy some, but I can't carry it around with me, for it would get all wrinkled up in my pockets, and besides, my pockets are loaded with coffee grounds and sugar and everything else a bum needs.

Besides writing a few letters to his friends, he mailed a series of postcards. In an era more than half a century before the invention of cell-phones, these cards assured his family that he was safe, somewhere within the 2,993,434 square miles of 1932 America. The cards also noted where he had been, town to town, allowing friends to keep a cumulative total of the number of miles he traveled. In addition, he received mail while on the road, his diary noting how he received letters addressed to him in care of General Delivery in Providence, Richmond, Brooksville (Florida), New Orleans, Memphis, and St. Paul.

It's too bad that no one had money to send him to augment his traveling budget, whose sum he included in an inventory taken on October 2, 1932 while in Aberdeen, South Dakota:

Right now I have 78 cents cash, 2 shirts, 2 pairs pants, 1 coat, 1 cap, 2 pairs of shoe strings, 4 books, cigarettes, papers, 1 sock, dukes mixture, pair goggles, new piece soap, lb coffee and sugar. The only thing I have on me when I left home is sweater and BVDs. All the other clothes are new to me, the pair of shoes I have on are 3 weeks from the store and the 4th pair since I left.

My father's writing and spelling are strikingly good, especially since his diary was written on park benches, in jails, missions, freight cars, and hobo jungles, by an eighth grade dropout whose parents spoke little English. He was a man who came to America as an infant, yet obviously developed a connection with his new country and a pride in it. In Richmond, Virginia, he wrote:

We went to look the town over from a to z. Saw the old capitol of the confederate states, saw the old St. John's church. Right in this church the famous Patrick Henry made his speech, Give me Liberty or give me Death. We stood for a minute in the exact same spot that old Pat stood in. This church was built in 1741. Later on we saw the grave spot of Elizabeth Arnold Poe, mother of Edgar Allen Poe, and the grave of George Wythe, the first professor of law in the U. States.

My father's familiarity with history is further evident in his September letter home from New Orleans:

I am exploring the Miss. River from south to north, and Joliet and LaSalle explored it from north to south. Well you see I'm different. And while I'm exploring I am also imploring my food.

CHAPTER 7
GETTING FED ON THE ROAD

Men eating in a homeless mission.
Photograph courtesy of The National Archives.

Imploring food was a top priority for Joe. All of the travel and adventure he anticipated depended upon him staying healthy and maintaining his strength and stamina. This, of course, meant he had to eat well. Malnutrition was a distinct threat during this time and the number of cases rose dramatically throughout the country, with transients especially vulnerable.

But, during the Depression, charities and soup kitchens helped provide a small safety net, making some food available for those in need. In Fort Wayne, Indiana, Joe wrote,

> *Looked all over town for supper and went to a hospital, got sandwiches and all the soup you can eat", and in Columbus, Ohio, "Went to a convent, had a bowl of soup.*

Soup kitchens and soup lines have endured as symbols of the Depression. In America's larger cities, the lines could stretch for blocks. In San Francisco, Joe recorded:

> *Went to a park in Columbia Square, washed up went to the soup line. About 2,000 guys in line, covered the whole block about 5 abreast, didn't go there anymore.*

This distressing sight of thousands of people waiting to be given small amounts of food, people capable and eager to work but with no place to be employed, inspired one of the hallmark songs of the era, *Breadline Blues*. This song, along with such others as *Brother, Can You Spare a Dime* and *Ain't Got No Home in This World Anymore*, reflected the melancholy mood of the time.

JOURNEY OF A DEPRESSION-ERA HOBO

Joe tried to avoid the soup lines, finding success soliciting handouts from private homes, restaurants, and butcher and baker shops. Numerous towns, however, discouraged such solicitation, and residents were told to refer the supplicants to a designated agency or facility.

Soup kitchen in Chicago, Illinois.
Photograph courtesy of The National Archives.

Often, the designated facility was the city hall. In Brattleboro, Vermont, Joe noted:

> *Well now we start to bum stores, but they all refused and said they give it to the city. Each and every butcher told us the same story. So we went to the city hall, cop said follow me, took us to a lunch car. Cop yelled at the top of his voice to the waiter give these guys coffee and rolls, the waiter gives us four donuts and cups of coffee each.*

BOARDING THE WESTBOUND

And, later,

Rode an empty to Pasco, Washington got there at 6 am to wait for the stores to open at 7. So I try to bum grub, all stores tell me to go to city hall.

In Eugene, Oregon,

I go uptown to bum some grub for the trip, the same old song, city hall.

Men being fed at the Salvation Army facility.
Photograph courtesy of The Salvation Army National Archives.

In other towns, those seeking handouts were directed to homeless missions or Salvation Army facilities, where transients could also receive sleeping quarters and baths. Joe wrote:

JOURNEY OF A DEPRESSION-ERA HOBO

So we are on the freight in an empty boxcar heading for Raleigh, North Carolina, get there at dinner time. Went to a couple of stores, they all direct you to the "Sally" [Salvation Army]...

Got to San Luis Obipso at 4 PM went to mooch, all send me to Sally...

Had to wait for the freight to Aberdeen, South Dakota, it was leaving at 10:30 am, so I grabbed it. Got to Aberdeen at 3-4 PM, started to bum houses for an afternoon luncheon, went to the towns 11 biggest houses, they all tried to send me to the Sally.

And, in Williams, Arizona,

I bummed a house, sends me to the mission, bummed a guy on the street, he also sends me to the mission.

Only once, on his last day on the road, did Joe incur a monetary charge at a mission or sally. Frequently, though, recipients had to perform some work. The work requirement likely could have been an enforcement of the anti-vagrancy concept, believing that everyone should earn his or her keep. In Richmond, Virginia, Joe wrote:

Then we went to the Sally, took a shower bath, went to bed at 9 PM. Got up at 6:30, had to work an hour for breakfast, I had to sweep the sidewalk and peel potatoes.

BOARDING THE WESTBOUND

In St. Paul, Minnesota:

Went to a mission, got breakfast, had to work for dinner, dust woodwork. For supper, I had to wait on tables, got a ticket for three meals.

In the neighboring city of Minneapolis:

More bums here than St. Paul. I went to the Union City mission to register, met a guy from Pittsburgh. I had to work 3 hours for supper, bed and breakfast, but since I was from Pittsburgh the guy said he would exempt me from work. He said it was good to talk to a guy from his old home town, it was lucky I knew the names of a few streets around Homewood.

In Hartford, Connecticut, in lieu of work, he had to participate in what some missions, mainly religiously-affiliated "rescue missions", required of their guests. Those served had to attend an in-house religious service, listen to a sermon, and sing religious songs. In Hartford, in the heat of summer, they sang outdoors on the roof:

Started to Hartford, got there alright. Went to a park, saw a baseball game, after the game went to a mission, had our supper. Sat around in the library and walked around town. Now it was time to sing on the roof, after singing we took a bath and went to bed.

JOURNEY OF A DEPRESSION-ERA HOBO

The safety net of the missions and sallies, the city halls, charities, and soup kitchens fulfilled the objective of providing basic sustenance, minimizing hunger and malnutrition. However, there would be places along Joe's 13,776-mile journey in which no safety net was available, and there would be times when he wanted more food, different food, better tasting and more nourishing.

The Salvation Army building at 32 Franklin Street in Columbus, Ohio in 1932. Joe slept there on December 2, 1932.

Photograph courtesy of The Salvation Army Archives.

BOARDING THE WESTBOUND

Although he praised the sally in Columbus, Ohio, ("Ate the best breakfast any sally puts out,") and the mission in Williams, Arizona, ("I Went to the mission, got toast, fried potatoes, best coffee I ever tasted in a soup house,") there were more cases where he found the meals wanting. About a mission in Jacksonville, Florida, he recorded:

> *I went to the American rescue workers, went down for my breakfast. Got dish of grit, grit is something new for me. I took one sip of it but did not like it, so I passed it to the man sitting next to me, he is crazy about grit.*

Then, in Pasco, Washington's city hall:

> *I went there, got some hot cakes, applesauce, I didn't eat any of that.*

And at the Eugene, Oregon City Hall:

> *I didn't like the stew, I started to walk out after I drank the milk. The cook yells, hey where you going, I said out. Well don't came back anymore if you don't want to eat, save it for somebody that does want to eat.*

The cook must have seen thousands of hungry people come through, probably few declining to eat like Joe, but more like the couple he noted, *I watched them put 2 stews apiece away.*

Not always liking what he was getting fed at city halls and missions, he solicited houses and food-related businesses for meals, and bummed for money on the streets. Besides providing him access to better meals, this brought Joe into contact with a variety of people. Eating in the city halls, and especially in the missions and sallies, put him predominately with the same people he met on the freights and in the hobo jungles. When bumming the streets, or soliciting houses and businesses, Joe was in touch with people from more diverse backgrounds. He encountered a wide range of responses, from hostility to kindness, from indifference to interest in his stories. He may not always have been a welcomed guest or companion, with his unshaven, sometimes dirty appearance, but his efforts were productive.

Many people had too little to be able to share anything and still others subscribed to the anti-vagrancy notion and disliked seeing people bumming on the streets.

In Forsyth, Montana,

> *5:30 PM, went uptown and all stores closed and no one parading the streets. I stood on a corner for a half hour, only 7 people pass me. I touched them all and only one was good for a dime...*

and,

> *Leave Raleigh 9 AM get to Hamlet, NC. at 2 PM. Hamlet is a very small town, about 500 people, tough bumming here, so we had to wait till 10 PM for a freight to Charleston, SC.*

BOARDING THE WESTBOUND

He wrote in Memphis,

Tried to bum dough, but nobody seems to have any.

Joe was in Memphis in September, and in September three years earlier, everybody seemed to have dough. *The Ladies Home Journal* printed an article titled, "Everybody Ought to be Rich", and the then soaring stock market was a major cause of that optimism with the U.S. Steel stock selling for $262 a share and Montgomery Ward stock selling for $148 a share. They were trading at $2 and $4 respectively when Joe began his trip, when the mood of the country reversed into the fear that everybody was going to be poor.

Some of the people he met were rude, perhaps stressed by their own meager finances, or possibly just overwhelmed by so many asking for handouts. In Spokane, Washington, he wrote:

I started to bum dough, got 40 cents, six nickels, one dime. Took about 2 hours, one guy very smart, said go home and see your ma...

In Brattleboro, Vermont,

Asked where we was from, we told him Pittsburgh. He said why the hell didn't you guys stay at home instead of bumming around.

And in Tallahassee, Florida,

JOURNEY OF A DEPRESSION-ERA HOBO

> ...*lady started to give me hell for bumming around and said why didn't I stay home. I did not pay much attention to her.*

Reports from this era tell of people putting signs on their houses that read, "Please do not knock, we have nothing for ourselves." Joe didn't encounter this, though he did write of people pretending they were not home by shutting off their radios upon hearing him approach.

Refusals from people who wouldn't, or couldn't, provide assistance weren't the only obstacles Joe encountered in his quest for handouts. In some locales, hobos were kept away through enforcement of vagrancy laws.

Joe experienced this early in the trip, in Alexandria, Virginia, where a local cop told him and Kelly to get off the streets: "*city cop comes around tells us to go to jungle.*" He constantly had to remain wary of this, but wasn't seriously bothered again by local police until much later, while in the southwestern region of the country. There, in four separate cities, Joe encountered a variety of threats and punishments by local authorities. In El Paso, Texas, a cop wanted him to leave a park:

> *I went to a park sat around pretty near all day. The park cop wanted to put me out. He saw my bundle and asked if I was traveling, I said yes. We started to talk, his name was Barker.*

BOARDING THE WESTBOUND

My father was thrown off the streets in one city in New Mexico and out of town in another. In Santa Fe, he wrote:

> *Got there about 10:30 and the cops stop me from a distance. They yelled wait a minute Chief, I waited, asked me where I was going, I told them Trinidad. They told me to keep off the streets.*

And in Albuquerque,

> *…just as soon as I got uptown the cops shake me down. Told me to get out of town, and I kept going, I didn't go out of town.*

Instead, he went to the sally, but returned to Albuquerque several days later, bravely, or foolishly, ignoring the cops' order to stay out of town.

It was especially brave, or foolish, considering what had happened to him a few weeks earlier in Las Vegas, Nevada. There, Joe was ordered out of town by a judge after the police jailed him for vagrancy, an arrest that would be mentioned in the local newspaper. Joe was locked up in a 1932 Las Vegas that would be unrecognizable today. Now an entertainment and gaming capital attracting more than ten million annual visitors, Las Vegas's population has increased one hundred fold from its 1930 level, and the county in which it resides, Clark, is now one of America's most populous. In 1932, the city's population was barely over 5,000 but it already had gambling facilities (legalized in 1931). This legalization coincided with the beginning of construction on the nearby Hoover Dam, and Las Vegas quickly become a source of entertainment and pleasure for the enormous workforce that was building the dam.

It was into this Las Vegas that Joe arrived in late October 1932:

> *I had dinner in the jungle, got the freight at 1 o'clock, went through Yermo then to Las Vegas at 1 AM after midnight, I slept on the freight coming in. Jumped off at Las Vegas, walked up main street about 2 blocks, got picked up and put in the brig. I was searched, took everything from my pockets then locked me up. There were 5 other prisoners before me, I slept till 8 o'clock, got oatmeal coffee and bread for breakfast. Well I thought I was getting 30 days when I got breakfast at 9 o'clock. I went up before the judge. He said you are charged with vagrancy, do you plead guilty or not. I plead not guilty, went on with the case in detail, so the Verdict was suspended till 9 o'clock next morning. Then they asked me if I could get out of town if they released me, I promised to get out of town on the first freight.*

But he stayed, immediately went uptown to bum, then to a casino,

> *I had 80 cents and started to play the craps. I lost 55¢ and quit and fell asleep under a table.*

BOARDING THE WESTBOUND

The next day, he showed some apprehension, but not much, about not having left town:

> *Since I was ordered out of town the day before I was almost afraid to go uptown but, I didn't care, I went up and bummed 45¢ and started to shoot craps. I won a dime and the guy asked me how old I was, I said 24, he didn't believe me, calls the cops, I ran out.*

This scared him, enough to leave town and the state, going to Utah, but he quickly returned:

> *So I got the freight at midnight, got into a reefer, spread my blanket and fell asleep. Got back to Las Vegas early in the morning Nov. 1, 1932, jungled up sweet rolls and coffee, monkeyed around the jungle all afternoon, washed my shirt. I picked up a newspaper and saw my name in it.*

> **PAIR FLOATED**
>
> George Cook and Joe Zulansky two itinerants bound from Los Angeles to eastern points, were ordered out of town this morning after pleading guilty to charges of vagrancy.

Las Vegas Newspaper
Pasted on the inside cover of Joe's 2nd notebook.

JOURNEY OF A DEPRESSION-ERA HOBO

In this incident, my father made light of what could have easily turned into a troublesome situation, 2,200 miles from home, stamped as an itinerant or vagrant, practically defenseless, without friends or advocates. His declining to leave after promising to obey the judge's order was disrespect of the law and could have brought harsh retaliation. Fortunately, nothing happened, and this was just another experience for him on his journey through America. The article referred to him as an itinerant, and trumpeted to readers that vagrants were being ordered out of town. Joe had been on the road for three full months before being arrested for vagrancy, having traveled through a number of states that either had no vagrancy laws, or if they did, didn't vigorously enforce them. These laws were remnants of a bygone era. But in 1932, in the Great Depression, the laws were obsolete and irrelevant with so few jobs available. While some never abandoned their beliefs in the principles of vagrancy laws, the prolonged hard times moved more people toward an understanding of the precarious situations of the indigent travelers. Some volunteered assistance, as in Las Vegas, New Mexico, where Joe recalled: *a fellow asked if I was on the road, I said yes sir. Well come on in, I ordered coffee and pie.* From Bainbridge, Georgia, he wrote:

> *I walked up to a house, knocked on the door and a big negro maid came to the door, wanted to know what I wanted. I told her, so she called the Mrs and the Mrs came. So I asked her if she could spare something for a hungry man, she said certainly. Told me to sit down*

> *on the steps, brings me out a big plate of sandwiches and some sliced pears and a glass of milk. She told me that wasn't much but I was welcome to it. I thanked her in a nice way.*

There were others who were caring, a few of whom Joe described as "big hearted." In Baldwin, Florida, he wrote,

> *This big-hearted Greek fried 3 eggs for me, 4 slices of bread, cup coffee and some vegetables, tasted good...*

and in a LaCrosse, Wisconsin restaurant,

> *...a big hearted customer said sit down lad take anything you want. I took hot cakes and syrup, coffee, I thanked him.*

Others, though not designated as big hearted, were just as generous. In Columbus, Ohio, Joe noted:

> *Saw the Ohio State Pen, walked around till I found the dormitories. Bummed a guy for a nickel, he said come with me. Took me to a high class restaurant, told me to take anything I like I ordered roast pork dinner.*

And in Manchester, New Hampshire:

> *Got there at 10:30 am, started to mooch stores. Got turned down at first store, 2nd store I asked the butcher for something to eat, he asked me if I was a hungry,*

> *I answered yes. So he took me to the restaurant next door and told the Greek to give me anything I wanted and he would pay for it. So I ordered 3 eggs sunny side up and 3 cups of coffee.*

The multiple references to Greeks reflect the extent to which members of this ethnic group became involved in the restaurant business, including owning several in Joe's hometown.

Like the butcher, a woman in Needles, California also questioned his hunger, and more, before giving anything:

> *The third house, the lady asked me if I was really hungry and penniless. I said lady if I wasn't hungry I wouldn't ask you, and if I had money I knew where to buy food. Although I had a dime, she didn't have to know it. She told me to sit down on the steps and in two minutes brings a big dish of sauerkraut and spare ribs, 4 boiled potatoes, half loaf bread and a cup of coffee. Then she said I guess you was hungry.*

In Aberdeen, South Dakota, a man seemingly familiar with the song Brother Can You Spare a Dime, gave Joe an extra nickel:

> *Saw a prosperous man, said Mack could you spare a hungry man a nickel, he gave me a dime...*

But in Tucumcari, New Mexico, the contributions stayed at the five cent level:

BOARDING THE WESTBOUND

...met a couple of good citizens, 2 of them gave me a nickel.

As charitable as these people were, the greatest generosity may have been extended by the very poor. In Bagdad, California, Joe recorded:

A little kid comes along, I told him to go home and tell his mother there is a boy in a car that didn't eat for three days. He went home, right next to this car I was sleeping in, his home was made out of a few boxcars. When he came back, he had a big bowl of cornflakes and hot milk some kind of Mexican biscuits, cup of coffee and a saucer, also bag full of dates. He said when I finished to bring the dishes to the house. I did, and his mother, a Mexican lady, gave me a bag of biscuits.

A home made of a boxcar.
Photograph courtesy of The National Archives.

JOURNEY OF A DEPRESSION-ERA HOBO

And near Tallahassee:

> Well, I went back to the shade tree, layed down, some pretty soon a small negro boy comes along, saw us cooking coffee. I asked him if his mother had any sugar, he said he would go home and find out. So he came back with a glass full of sugar and some biscuits. I tell him I would tattoo him for it with this indelible pencil, so another guy put a star on his arm. And another Negro kid was there and we knew his name was James, so this other kid said, gee I wish I could get a star on my arm. And I told him to go home and bring some biscuits, gee did he run home for some food, came back with a poke full of biscuits, corn bread and a piece of cake. Well he got a star tattooed on his arm, was he proud of the tattooed arm, told him it would never come off his arm.

In Albuquerque, New Mexico, he wrote:

> I went to the stockyards, met a little Spanish kid, told him to go home to get me some coffee. He went right home came back in five minutes with a pint of hot coffee and couple of torteos sandwiches.

Joe did quite well in his search for money and food, receiving help from a cross section of people, from a prosperous man in South Dakota to a woman living in boxcars in California. Many others, while generous, required him to earn what he received. In exchange for meals, he chopped wood, pulled weeds, washed windows, and unloaded gravel. In Klamath Falls, Oregon, he noted:

> *Went uptown and hit a house, put me to work chopping wood. Got a steak dinner, soup, peas, tomatoes, gravy, with tea, all the steak I could eat, I ate 3 big slices. I found out her husband worked in a butcher shop. So she told me to chop some more, and I did, thought I was going to get some money. But I get surprised and didn't get any money but some more steak in a bag—steak sandwiches.*

He pulled weeds in Hannibal, Missouri, the boyhood home of Mark Twain:

> *Had to pull weeds from sidewalk, got 5 sandwiches, two glasses of milk, two apples, pair of socks, one sack bull Durham.*

In Las Vegas, Nevada, right after being ordered out of town at his 9:00 hearing, Joe wrote:

> *I was hungry and went to a house at 9:30 o'clock, rapped on the door asked the lady for a bite to eat. She asked me if I could wash windows and I said yes, told me to wait till she fixed something for me, 5 strips bacon and 2 eggs, coffee. Then I started to wash the windows, she said maybe you want a smoke after breakfast and I said yes, and I had plenty of smoking*

> *tobacco. Well she handed me 3 lucky strikes. I went on and washed six windows. She asked me if I had any more cigarettes and I said no, oh mister you are smoking too many cigarettes, but she smoked 5 to my three and hollering me smoking too much.*

And near Springfield Massachusetts:

> *We were getting hungry, walked to a farmer's house, Kelly approached the farmer for a bite to eat. The farmer said sure, if you will help me for a few minutes. OK we worked and he had a wagon load of gravel to be leveled over the drive-way, took ten min to do it. In the meantime the lady farmer was frying 3 eggs apiece.*

He also did some work for meals in restaurants, baker shops, a schoolhouse, and hotels, including, appropriately, on Labor Day:

> *I went to the rear of the hotel, one of the biggest in Tallahassee and asked for something to eat. She said you have to chop some wood, I said O.K well took about ten minutes to chop the wood. Then I sat down to my supper, oh boy a big plate full of chipped kidney meat and some other kind of meat, mixed potatoes, lettuce, sliced tomatoes and great big glass of iced tea and a piece of lemon. Pretty good feed for a bum on Labor Day.*

BOARDING THE WESTBOUND

There was more wood chopping in Bagdad, California:

It is 3 o'clock in the afternoon Friday November 4. School is over at 3:30 and I went up and put the bum on the school teacher, she made me chop wood for 15 minutes then called me in to eat. She ate right with me, had stew.

It was box splitting in Winslow, Arizona:

I went to the biggest café in town, he made me split boxes and take the nails out and I did that easy enough, I got hot cakes extra large and 2 eggs, 2 cups coffee…,

and floor mopping in Marmath, North Dakota:

Man sweeping the restaurant floor, I said I could do it for a cup of a coffee. He said he would sweep, asked me if I could mop, I said sure so I mopped the floor. He gave me 3 hot cakes, 2 fried eggs, 2 cups coffee, I put that away alright.

Joe cleaned pans in LaCrosse, Wisconsin:

Walked into a baker shop, asked for something, the lady asked me if I can work, I said sure if I can find any. Well she said go to the rear and help the baker, I had to clean about 42 pans, came to the lady again,

JOURNEY OF A DEPRESSION-ERA HOBO

told I was finished working so she gave me about 6 pounds of mixed cakes, jelly rolls, buns and donuts.

Though willing to work, Joe opted out when possible. In Fulton, Kentucky, he wrote:

Then a truck came by and was going to the cinder pile, he whistled for me, I came down. He asked me if I wanted to make a little change or tobacco money, I said yes. I took the shovel and he went to the round house, said he would be back about 20 minutes. Well I shoveled 5 shovels and another guy came around and said he wanted to help me, I said I would give him a dime for a loading the truck, he said alright. So he started to pile the truck to the top, it was a 1 ton truck so the truck was loaded, I gave him a dime, he was glad. The truckman gave 30 cents for the job, well I made 4 cents on a shovelful.

Twice, he did agree to take jobs, working for half a day in Omaha, Nebraska and accepting an offer in Maryland as a ploy to get supper and a night's lodging. In Omaha,

…got a job in a second hand clothing store, started at 1 o'clock quit at 5. This is the reason I quit. I got two bits for working, he told me to come back the next day I didn't go.

BOARDING THE WESTBOUND

Getting paid twenty-five cents for four hours work didn't appeal to him, not when he made twenty cents for shoveling five shovelfuls of cinders, not when he was getting well-fed for doing chores that took only ten to fifteen minutes, and not when he could get money just by bumming on the streets.

His other job was an interesting one, at a large dog kennel in Elkridge, Maryland. When a man giving them a ride from Baltimore to Washington got a flat tire on his truck, Joe and Kelly got out and started walking alongside U.S. Route 1:

> *Kelly walked yards away from me, stopped at a dog zoo, look at dogs for a while. The boss met him and asked if he was looking for a job, Kelly said yes sir and I have a buddy up street, will you have 2 of us. Boss said sure Kelly whistled for me and I came down Boss said if I wanted to work too, I said yes sir. Well he took us all over this kennel, told us what we had to do. Here is what he said: get up at 6 AM, milk the cows, come in eat breakfast, go out clean manure from 500 dogs, cut weeds, feed dogs, water them, and do one thing or another all day long till it gets dark and only 1 dollar a week. Well it is about 4 PM and we are getting hungry, I asked if he would give us supper today, oh sure said he. Well we decided to stay for supper at least. Well, we said we would work. He said we could wash our clothes and take a shower bath, we took advantage of both. I washed my shirt, BVD's, pants, and socks, they*

> had a 492 model washing machine, put the clothes out under the sun. Walked around the farm eating pears and looking at all the dogs, then we were called in for supper. Got hamburger, sliced tomatoes, potatoes, gravy, peas, bread, butter and milk. So we began to talk about our new job with the new boss, he asked how long we expected to stay on the job, we told him all winter. He said he was looking for someone who would work for him all year, we said if we liked it we would stay all our lives, farmer said to his wife. By God, these 2 men are real good workers. You know we told him about how long we stayed on the job we had before depression, so he liked to hear us tell about ourselves, and we were talking so much I thought we would get a raise in salary before we started to work.

Before going to bed, to rest for the next day's work, the beginning of professed lifelong careers at the dog kennel, they entertained the farmer's daughter and a couple of their new co-workers. Then, since work was to begin early, they retired for the night:

> Well it is 9:30 and time for the farmers to go to bed they went to bed, bid me and Kelly goodnight and said I will see you in the morning. We said goodnight right after the old folks went to bed, we know the farmer is getting up it 6 AM, well we said we would get up at

BOARDING THE WESTBOUND

daybreak and run away. Boy we slept like a log till 5:30 and the farmer was up too. We went around, got our clothes from the line, we got up around the other side of the barn ran through tall grass corn and weeds and started for Washington. This was all we wanted was supper and a place to sleep.

Joe managed to obtain some of the kennel's letterhead, and used it for a letter he wrote from Richmond to friends back home.

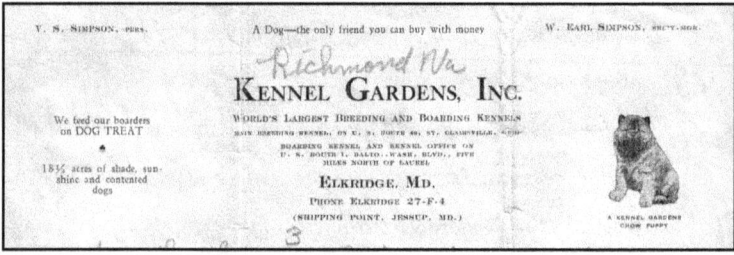

The letterhead Joe obtained from Kennel Gardens, Inc.

Even if Joe had been serious about being willing to work there for the rest of his life, the job would have been short-lived. By 1935, the business was gone and the property turned into one of the world's first pet cemeteries. The cemetery still exists today alongside Route 1, and now allows people to be buried next to their animal companions.

JOURNEY OF A DEPRESSION-ERA HOBO

There are two houses still there. The one shown is where the workers slept, including Joe and Kelly on August 22, 1932. The structure on the right of the picture is the owners house just off of Route 1 near Laurel, Maryland.

This ruse helped net a good meal, and he went beyond this once in his quest for food, stealing some in Florida. In a town near Jacksonville, Florida, Joe wrote:

> *And I went to this small town and bum something to eat. I went to 14 or 16 houses, couldn't get anything except 2 cheese sandwiches, well I thought two sandwiches wasn't enough so I went to the town's biggest hotel. Rapped on the back door but nobody answers my rapping, well I looked around and saw two big home made pies and six quarts of jelly. Well nobody answers. Now I will take one pie and one quart of jelly, I took pie and a quart of jelly, jumped over the rear fence and went up the alley for a block and started*

up the RR tracks, found a nice spot to sit down and I had a nice little lunch.

This was the only time Joe stole food on the trip, but it was not uncommon among the wandering homeless. The offenders, probably law-abiding in better times, took from others, primarily farmers and shopkeepers. Many were scared, seeing first-hand on a daily basis a dark side of life on the open road and the ever-present menace of chronic hunger. The extent of malnutrition during the Depression has been well documented by statistics. The numbers were depressing, some particularly so, such as the report that one-fifth of the children in New York City were malnourished. The pitiable feelings evoked by statistics couldn't match those caused by seeing the reality that they reflected. One report told of a New York schoolteacher telling a hungry child to go home and eat, only to have the child reply, "I can't, this is my sister's day to eat."

JOURNEY OF A DEPRESSION-ERA HOBO

The children weren't going hungry on Thanksgiving Day, 1932. The Salvation Army held a dinner at a New York hotel for children of destitute families.
Photograph courtesy of The Salvation Army National Archives.

Few things can generate sympathy and pity like images of hungry children, but this dreaded malnutrition was even more of a threat to transients, who were usually out of reach of any potential assistance. Becoming ill created precarious circumstances for hobos, removed from caring family and friends, in an environment where hospitals were giving preference to the overflowing number of ailing from the local community.

Fortunately, malnutrition and chronic hunger were never problems for my father, who, instead, sometimes received too much to eat. He described one typical day:

>   ...*started for Marion, Arkansas got to Marion at 11 AM, ate dinner at a house, got a big sit down.*

And he experienced days such as in Montevideo, Minnesota when he,

> ...ate too much had to lay down a while and give stomach a rest...

and in Dubuque, Iowa,

> Went to a restaurant got a big sit down, oh a big plate of meat, mashed potatoes, and cabbage coffee, oh I could hardly walk after I ate.

It may have been even better in Richmond, Virginia:

> Had a good supper, we could only eat about half of it, gave the other half away to 3 lady bums, two husbands and 1 baby...

and after being delayed, got some more:

> So the train was late and we got 2 more watermelons, Boy oh Boy this is the place for watermelon. So we gave one whole watermelon to the lady bums, ate another half and gave half to a couple other bums. What a feast, what a feast.

These seemed surprising words from a man in his circumstances. Occasionally he shared his bounty. In Philadelphia he recorded:

JOURNEY OF A DEPRESSION-ERA HOBO

We started to monkey around under the bridge met a Negro from North Carolina, gave him some eats we had left over.

Hobos sharing food.
Photograph courtesy of The Library of Congress.

And from Dubuque, Iowa:

I got too much today, I gave some to the other bums at the jungle…

and in Miles City, Montana:

…got 9 eggs boiled at a house, well I shared my eggs with a guy.

BOARDING THE WESTBOUND

A defining moment occurred in San Francisco, where food came to him:

> *It was about 11 o'clock and I was right in the heart of town, got a big bag of cakes at bakery. About a block down at Howard and 4th Street a big truck loses a case of eggs, I was the second one out in the middle of the street to get a share of the eggs. About 3/4 of the case were all broken up the middle of the street, was all yellow and slippery, I filled my soldiers cap, all could fit in it was 22. Got coffee at a house, jungled up saved about 9 eggs, hard boiled, for the ride.*

While food almost fell on him in San Francisco, it didn't in Philadelphia, where Joe described Kelly, the fellow from North Carolina, and himself:

> *We were sitting under the bridge, someone walked above us on the bridge, threw an empty pie plate, the Negro looked up and said Oh Lord Oh Lord send me down a pie, I know you made more when you made that one. The Lord did not respond.*

Perhaps in an effort to further implore the Lord, the trio held a religious service led by the man from North Carolina.

> *He told us he used to go to school and took up preaching, one more year and would have been a deacon, but he*

said he quit goin to church. He sang a couple of hymns, later he started to preach a Negro Service.

Again, no response, but despite the Lord's failure to send pie from the sky, Joe was eating pretty well, and his next major pursuit was for places to sleep.

CHAPTER 8
PLACES TO SLEEP

Cots in a Salvation Army in Chicago, Illinois.
At night, sleeping quarters in most Salvation Armys were filled to capacity.
Courtesy of The Salvation Army National Archives.

Like Joe, some people on the road were homeless by choice, but others were cruelly uprooted, having lost their homes and their farms in the Depression. Among these inexperienced travelers, cases of pneumonia and tuberculosis mounted, brought on in part by prolonged exposure to the cold and rain. Shelter was necessary, but proper rest was also vital.

Just as missions and sallies could provide a basic meal when one was truly needed, they also offered shelter—a bed, or cot, and usually a bath. In a letter dated September 18 Joe wrote:

> *Often times I sleep in a mission for 2 or 3 days to land a soft place to sleep.*

Among the dozens of missions and sallies where he slept, he described "a nice soft hotel bed" in Portland, Oregon. In Providence, Rhode Island, he noted:

> *Now it is Monday August 15 started for Providence, got there at 6 PM bummed ham, buns and cake, went to park and stayed in park to 9:00 then went to flop house. Went to bed at 11:00 up at 5:30 am walked around town waiting for PO to open, PO opened at 7:30 got the mail so we went to another mission and ate.*

The large increase in the number of homeless strained the capacities of these refuges. From Jacksonville, Florida, Joe wrote:

> Then went to the office of the Sally, send me back to the registering room which was about 10 blocks, after I get there the rooms were all occupied.

And in Marion, Ohio:

> Went to the sally took a bath and a nice clean place to sleep, almost got turned down here.

In efforts to ration their available rooms, missions and sallies limited the number of nights each person could stay. Joe's September 18 letter noted:

> I stay till they tell me to keep moving, in other words you run your lease.

He was told to keep moving in Spokane, Washington, where a brewery (banned from operation during Prohibition) was used as a homeless shelter:

> Stopped at the DeGink Old Schade Brewery, took a bath, went uptown, started to rain had to come back, bummed eats. Wouldn't let me stay 2nd night at the DeGink, I went to an old barn in the fairgrounds, pretty chilly.

Preferring missions to chilly nights, Joe found ways to stay longer. In Omaha, Nebraska, he recorded:

BOARDING THE WESTBOUND

Got to Omaha at midnight went to police station, gave me a ticket for Sally.

The next night, when he was no longer welcome, he wrote:

...pretty cold tonight and I had to sleep somewhere so I went to the Sally, gave them another fictitious name, they didn't know the difference.

He did the same in El Paso, Texas:

Went back to the Sally they allow only one night so I had to give a bogus monniker.

Sleeping indoors kept Joe from the chill and the cold, but these missions, filled with exhausted, sleeping men, didn't always offer a comforting atmosphere. The men slept in rooms crowded with beds and cots, and some, possibly disturbed, slept fitfully.

JOURNEY OF A DEPRESSION-ERA HOBO

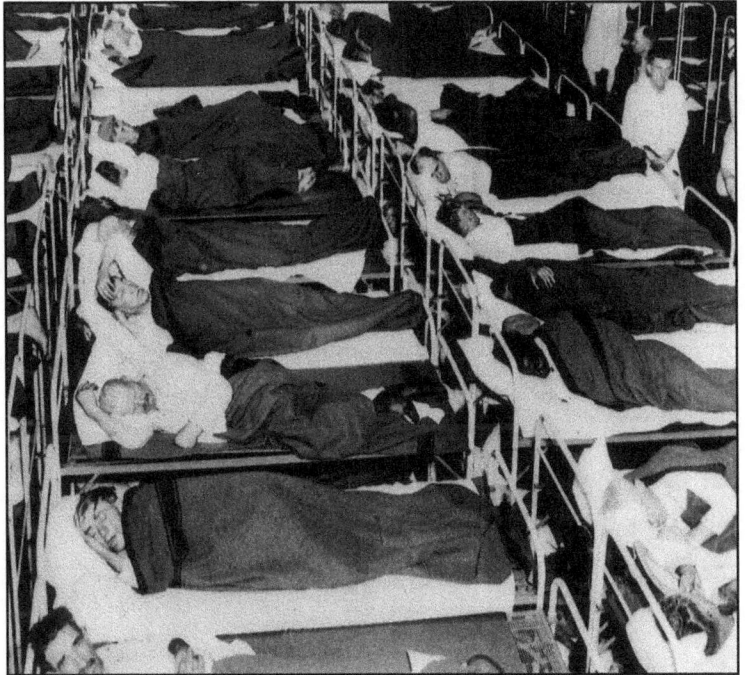

Men sleeping in a shelter for the unemployed in New York City.
Photograph courtesy of The National Archives.

In St. Paul, Minnesota mission, Joe wrote:

Some guy was talking in his sleep everything so quiet at 2 AM so I was scared when he started to talk. Later I laughed when I found out where it came from...

In a mission in New Orleans:

...fell asleep OK, some guy started to talk in his sleep woke everybody up.

BOARDING THE WESTBOUND

At the Memphis sally he noted,

> *...took a bath went to sleep at 11 PM, about 11:30 a man starts moaning and talking in his sleep, everybody got up.*

Then,

> *...line up for breakfast and they ask you your name, so one guy forgot his.*

This man may have been physically worn, or mentally troubled, or both. An observer of out of work people traveling through the country looking for jobs in this era wrote:

> *There were hardly any jobs, however far a-field they traveled. So they found themselves drifting around aimlessly, cursing at themselves, and becoming more demoralized and wondering where the hell they go from here. It was sad to see humanity in this state.*

> (Source: Bill Bailey, *The People's Century*)

While this was likely visible in some of the people Joe saw in the missions and sallies, on the freight and in the jungles, it didn't characterize him. My father wasn't demoralized or drifting aimlessly; he was on the adventure of a lifetime.

Though more vulnerable there, Joe enjoyed sleeping outdoors when conditions were acceptable. Outside Tallahassee, he wrote:

> *So I went to a saw mill went to sleep at the lumber camp slept on saw dust shavings till 7:00 AM, pretty good place to sleep.*

He even slept outdoors in major cities. From New York City he recorded:

> *We went to sleep under a viaduct on a newsstand, got up at 8:30.*

And, later:

> *Crossed the river into St. Louis MO, walk around take in all the sights, bummed a restaurant got a good feed, came under the bridge again went to sleep.*

In California:

> *It is 2 o'clock in the morning and I hit the city limits of Los Angeles went under a bridge to finish the nights sleep.*

In addition to big cities, Joe slept outdoors in the country's wide-open spaces, including the desert. In Barstow, California, he noted:

> *So I had to find a nice place to sleep so I slept in a sand house…*

BOARDING THE WESTBOUND

And in Las Vegas, Nevada:

> *Shot Craps, lost all and now I am broke happy and satisfied, went to sleep in the desert on the sand.*

In further contrast to the demoralized, Joe was experiencing one of life's cherished moments, feeling at peace with the world and his place within it. He had no money, but no matter, he was content.

Joe enjoyed the serenity of sleeping alone outdoors. Only once did he sleep in one of the hobo jungles. These jungles—campsites built near rail yards—were meeting places for travelers, sites where they could build fires to heat coffee and food, trade stories, and relax among fellow road people.

Joe would hear stories from people who lived a lifestyle in which all time was free time, different than the one from which he was taking a brief respite, one of commitment to family and work. He would listen to people who spent much of their adult lives riding the rails, traveling to places that those bound by relationships would rarely or never see. They are part of a distinctive, somewhat mysterious culture, people unwilling to live under the standard norms of mainstream society, tired to living up to others' expectations. Along with freedom and independence, they value and respect privacy, preferring to be known almost exclusively by their nicknames and traveling names, and leaving outsiders to wonder whether they've been living on the road solely to answer the call of adventure, or to escape a troubling life situation.

The jungle he slept in was in Vicksburg, Mississippi:

> *Went to the jungle made coffee, ate a good supper, had some left over for the next day, made another fire at midnight, boiled some more coffee went to sleep got up at 5:30 freight leaving for Memphis at 6.*

Of course, his nights outside were sometimes limited by nature. In New Orleans, he wrote:

> *Well it is 10 PM and I want to sleep outdoors but the mosquitoes are busy tonight, I went back to the mission.*

He slept in a barn in chilly Spokane, Washington after being denied a second might at the brewery. In Niles, Michigan, he noted:

> *Got there at 9 o'clock, too cold to ride. I found an old shanty, had a stove in it, went out got some waste from the grease boxes and a pile of coal, it got nice and warm in a few minutes. I stretched out on the floor never got my eyes open till about 8:00 o'clock.*

When other choices were unavailable, Joe at various times checked in at the local jail. These visits were voluntary, not at the insistence of the local authorities as in Las Vegas. Typically, he had a cell for a night's sleep and breakfast in the morning. He wrote:

BOARDING THE WESTBOUND

> *Rode to Boone, Iowa went to the jail slept 16 hours and had breakfast in jail.*

In Newark, Ohio, he noted:

> *…rode to Newark got off at 10:30 went to jail to sleep got up at 8 o'clock ate breakfast…*

And in Marmath, North Dakota,

> *…went to jail slept till 7:15 AM this is Wednesday morning Oct. 6.*

This arrangement wasn't guaranteed, as not all communities welcomed transients into their jails. In Alexandria, Virginia, where earlier in the day police had told him to leave the streets and go to the jungle, he described:

> *Well, we go into the police station to try to get a place to sleep but they turned us down so we go and look for an empty boxcar. We found a nice one to sleep in, lots of paper…*

And in Wisconsin,

> *Got to LaCrosse at 8:00 PM, went to police station, turned me away so I found a box car with a lot of paper made myself a nice bed and fell asleep at 10 PM get up at 9 AM, never slept so long yet.*

JOURNEY OF A DEPRESSION-ERA HOBO

While some jails were off-limits to people on the road, others set themselves up specifically to assist the growing number of transients, as Joe noted:

> *Got to Milford, Utah at midnight went to jail and I found some cans and made coffee then went to sleep, town Marshall comes in at 7:00 in the morning wakes me up said there is a freight going in my direction. I didn't get up, slept till eight o'clock, they have a special place in this town for bums only this old jail house.*

In Brattleboro, Vermont, he wrote:

> *Got to talking with a bunch of local boys got some information about lodging. They suggested police station so we went there about 9 PM we were placed in good cells, two blankets and cushion, so we fell asleep immediately. And at eleven PM night crew came on duty, there was another bum in the cell with us, local bum, so the chief says alright boys downstairs and this is the place for bums to sleep, downstairs. And the chief gave a second look at this local bum and told him to get the hell out and punched him in the back of the head and kicked him in the seat of his pants and told him don't let me see you around this jail anymore and it was plenty cold that night too. So we watched all the cop did and started to laugh, turned to us and said where you guys from, we told him, well get downstairs*

BOARDING THE WESTBOUND

and sleep with the rest of the bums. We went downstairs about ten guys laying on cots and sleeping.

While hospitable, these jails accommodated men who may have been on the road, unable to wash for days, and saw conditions that were at times less than sanitary. In Brattleboro, my father noted:

One guy came about 15 minutes, said he couldn't sleep too darn many bedbugs biting. He picked up a few and showed them to us, we decided to get out of this and sleep in a boxcar.

The boxcar provided both transportation and a place to sleep.

Joe spent the majority of his nights on the road in boxcars, and they became the closest thing to a home away from home. The ones in Brattleboro, Alexandria, and LaCrosse were stationary in the rail yards, and he noted:

JOURNEY OF A DEPRESSION-ERA HOBO

...when you are in a still boxcar it is more enjoyable.

When riding, my father sought empty cars, a luxury in some ways compared to a mission with rooms full of weary men. Several times, Joe noted that he slept through his destination:

> *The car had a couple old sacks so I rolled them up and made a pillow and fell asleep. Well, I slept like a dead man. I was supposed to get off at Tallahassee but the freight went through Tallahassee while I was asleep...*

> *Met a couple other guys, talked for a while and the freight was coming so I hopped on and wanted to get off at Biloxi, Mississippi but I fell asleep on the freight, never awoke till it go to New Orleans...*

> *Caught a freight going north, I wanted to get off at Trinidad but I fell asleep under my blanket, it was pretty cold and I wrapped myself in the blanket, when I awoke I was on my way to Denver.*

Chapter 9
RAILROAD BULLS

Cop chasing boy in railyard.
Railroad companies employed their own policemen whose responsibilities included keeping the rail yards free of hobos and other trespassers.
Photograph courtesy of the Carnegie Library of Pittsburgh.

Joe and thousands of others who availed themselves of freight cars were unwelcome intruders. Riding the freights was illegal, and the railroad cops reminded Joe of this. While in a refrigerator car in New Mexico, he wrote:

> *The name of this town is Tucumcari I crawled into a reefer, the bull puts me out, he said what the hell do you think this is, a hotel car.*

Near Bagdad, California, he described:

> *I saw him putting an old man off then he came to me. I couldn't get away no how, flashed the light on me frisked me, and said don't you now you are violating the law by riding the freight.*

The bulls, employees of the railroad lines, worked in the rail yards and rode the trains, both to prevent damage and theft of railroad property and to rid trains of freeloading riders. They dealt quickly and harshly with anyone attempting destruction or theft, as Joe noted in Kansas City, Missouri:

> *I saw a bull shoot at two bums—they were monkeying with seals.*

Bulls were more lenient in their treatment of vagrant riders. Illegal though it was, the majority of railroad cops weren't eager to jail transients. This was fortunate for the judicial system, as courts and jails would have been overflowing. The bulls usually contented themselves with kicking hobos off the trains and keeping then out of the rail yards, duties they performed with varying degrees of enthusiasm. Expulsion was usually sufficient, and necessary, since more than being nuisances, hobos could be safety hazards, with the Texas Madman (chosen Grand Duke of the Hobos at a recent Britt, Iowa Hobo Convention) pointing out the majority of train derailments were caused by "hobos monkeying around."

To avoid the bulls, illegal riders would scout the train yards, pinpoint the desired train's location, its scheduled time to leave, and try to keep out of sight until immediately before its departure. These maneuvering led to a continuous game of hide and seek between bull and traveler.

In the railyards, hobos would have to find the schedule, locate the train they wanted, and avoid the bulls.

Photograph courtesy of the Carnegie Library of Pittsburgh.

BOARDING THE WESTBOUND

In Richmond, Virginia, my father noted:

So it was time for the freight to pull out, it was pulling out and 2 bulls watched that no one got on, so the next freight was going to leave at 4 am.

And in Barstow, California, he wrote:

Tried to get on same freight but got kicked out of the yards, the same bull meets me again asks me where I am going I said Las Vegas, you going to buy a ticket, I said no, well get the hell out of here.

In Baldwin, Florida, he recorded:

Sat on the depot for a while waiting for a freight and a half hour before the freight was due the Old Bull showed his face and I ducked into the tall grass.

A successful boarding didn't end the cat and mouse games, as bulls continually patrolled moving trains to seek out and evict illegal travelers. In Tallahassee, Florida, Joe wrote:

I hopped on stayed on 5 min and got kicked off so I ran to the back and hopped on again. Well he followed me back and said get the hell off and stay the hell off, well I did get off, tried again but he was watching too close so I stayed the hell off for good.

JOURNEY OF A DEPRESSION-ERA HOBO

These "games" could get dangerous, as they were played on fast-moving freights. Joe described traveling from Caliente, Nevada to Milford, Utah in a refrigerator car:

> ...got into a reefer got kicked out about 50 miles from Caliente so I had to ride the tops for 20 miles...

and en route to Needles, California:

> I jumped on top of a car and hid, riding the tops until arriving in the Needles freight yard.

View showing tops of boxcars, where hobos would sometimes ride to hide from the bulls.

Photograph courtesy of The National Archives.

BOARDING THE WESTBOUND

During these pursuits by the bulls, Joe experienced some satisfaction in eluding them. In Baldwin, Florida, he noted:

> *Pretty soon the freight came in and I started down toward the water tank, so the freight stopped for water and I walked alongside the freight looking for an empty box car. As I was walking on one side the old bull was walking down the other side of the freight, so he saw me and flashed his light on me and hollered come back here and I started to run as fast as my feet could carry me. So I found a box car jumped in It, got my clothes all white then lighted a match and found out it had hauled flour. Well I saw the old bull pass me, he never looked in the car I was in so I jumped out found another car, it was nice and clean.*

Bulls could be eluded, and at times weren't even on board, otherwise a trip of nearly fourteen thousand miles couldn't have happened. But when they were on the prowl, they typically won the skirmishes. From Columbus, Ohio, Joe wrote:

> *I tried to go to Newark, Ohio, hopped the first freight, rode four miles out. On top of a hill, four bulls searched the freight, they found me between two cars and said get the hell off and stay off the RR property. I got off and ran thru a farmer's field, the farmer started to call me off his field and I kept running till I got way up by the engine. The freight was moving now, I jumped*

about five fences till I got about 10 feet from the track, and I heard a couple of shots. I looked around, on top of a car a bull was looking at me and he motioned to stay off. I walked down to the yards again, hopped on another, got to the same place this time I was in a low gondola between sewer pipes.

They found me again and said they meant it when they say to keep off. I showed them my cards, but they wouldn't let me on.

Joe gave no description of the cards, but one that some hobos carried and probably didn't show to bulls was a membership card in the "One Big Union." This was a remnant from the pre-Depression era when everyone was expected to have a job, when hobos who drifted from casual occupation to casual occupation became part of the "I Won't Work Movement," also known as the "One Big Union."

Joe was never arrested for riding freights. Nonetheless, the arrest for vagrancy in Las Vegas wasn't his first encounter with a judge. Barely two weeks into the trip, while in New England, he and Kelly were arrested for riding a passenger train without tickets or the means to pay for them. During the course of their legal proceedings, they saw another group of men receive jail sentences for riding freights. Joe quickly saw that excitement, or trouble, could appear anytime, anywhere, along the way.

BOARDING THE WESTBOUND

This first legal encounter occurred in Portland, Maine, at the end of a ride that began innocently enough. According to the diary entry from Dover, New Hampshire:

> *About 100 girls from a shoe factory, got acquainted with about 15 girls that worked there, all French girls, had lots of fun joking with them.*

After lunch, it was to the railroad yards, where Kelly and my father sneaked onto a passenger train:

> *Riding right behind the engine, all set for Portland, Maine. Made 2 or 3 stops and landed at Portland station with a bull and station master waiting to greet us. I saw the bull and started up the avenue at full speed, was whole block from the bull when he grabbed Kelly. So Kelly yelled at me and I came up to the bull, he asked our names and where we got the train, etc. then the conductor came along and demanded the fare from Dover to Portland—$1.62 each. Told him we didn't have it, so the bull marched us up to the depot, one-hundred people looking at us, the bull called the patrol buggy. We rode through the town, stopped at the jail, unloaded us, locked us up, gave us two biscuits, couple cups of water, Kelly sang a few songs. We spent 24 cents for two packages of cigarettes and about 11 PM we fell asleep, got up at seven, waited for 9 AM for court. Court opens at 9, a few cases before ours,*

we listened to the other cases one was comic. A social leader pinched for disturbing peace, he acts as his own lawyer, also has another charge against him. He outsmarted the city attorney on one charge, but got 30 days for disturbing peace. He appealed for new trial, got one too. He had a Jew for his witness, the Jew didn't know his name so he finally said his name was Nathan Innebenne, occupation was peddler, he had to spell his name couple times before anybody could understand it. Next came six Negros pinched for riding freight, each got 20 days. Then Kelly's and mine, this is Verdict: five bucks fine, six months' parole. So we didn't have to pay $5.00, probation officer makes out our parole cards and asks when did we eat last. Of course we told him two days ago, he was big hearted and slipped us a buck, we thanked him, went to the Post Office mailed cards home, saw Atlantic Ocean.

With their fine forgiven, and the receipt of a dollar from the probation officer, they did pretty well. They got a ride to Portland, a night's sleep, and some entertainment. Kelly sang in jail and they watched the trials that proceeded theirs as though they were watching a show. The social leader was serious, likely one of the growing numbers of Americans in 1932 who were calling for more government action to alleviate suffering caused by the Depression, many advocating outright socialism. As for Joe and Kelly, there were no signs of seriousness or anxiety, only signs of enjoyment, enjoying the comic trial, enjoying viewing the Atlantic Ocean.

Less than a month later my father would again get caught on a passenger train, this time spared from arrest and merely thrown off the train.

In Tallahassee, Florida, he wrote:

> *Found what time the next freight was going out, none till next morning at 9 o'clock and the next train was leaving at 3 PM. Well I wait till 3 PM and hopped on this passenger train and a few more got on, so the engineer saw the last man get on, went about 20 feet, stopped the train and kicked all of us off. What tough luck.*

Although illegal riders were called vagrants by the legal system and itinerants by the some newspapers, the public had their own terms: hobos, tramps, or bums. Most people had a tendency to lump them all into the same category, and any given person apt to use different terms at different times. But serious observers of Hobo culture, like author Roger Bruns, differentiate among these terms and offer a strict definition of each.

Bruns in his book, *Knights of the Road—A Hobo History*, defines a hobo as a migratory worker not wanting anything for nothing; a tramp as a migratory non-worker, a professional idler; and a bum as a nonmigratory, non-worker harboring an aversion to work.

JOURNEY OF A DEPRESSION-ERA HOBO

Joe met the criteria of a hobo. His many thousands of miles of rail travel qualified him as migratory, he worked for food and shelter when necessary, and his time before and after the Depression showed no aversion to work. However, the distinctions between hobos, tramps, and bums were blurred during the Depression. Joe referred to himself and fellow travelers most frequently as bums, although he and the others did work.

The most popular person riding the rails in those years was the fictional character created by Charlie Chaplin called the Little Tramp. For a nation seeking escape from hard times, the Little Tramp provided relief, and the public cared less about whether he was known as a tramp, hobo, or bum. He made them laugh, and his imagined lifestyle, on the open road with few cares, offered further escape.

CHAPTER 10
LOOKING LIKE A HOBO

Hobos of various ages keeping warm at the Salvation Army
in Memphis, Tennessee.

Photograph courtesy The Salvation Army National Archives.

Somewhere behind the adventure and excitement was the unexciting, unadventurous effort to maintain at least a minimal level of cleanliness and hygiene. Its importance is shown by this inclusion into the Hobo Code: "Try to stay clean and boil up when possible." "Boiling up" meant washing with water boiled in the hobo jungles, but for most the daily routine—walking through towns, working for meals, long hours in dirty boxcars, and prolonged exposure to streams of dirty smoke spewing from coal-fueled engines, made cleanliness a difficult, nearly impossible end. In his diary, Joe noted in Salem, Oregon:

> *A lady, 2 kids about 3 and 1 years old with her hubby comes in to eat. Dirty as pigs, I pitied them…,*

and

> *…walked down to the RR yards, met a lady bum, she was about 26 years of age and dirtier than I ever was. She was going to St. Petersburg, and this is Flomaton, Ala.*

Mission and sallies usually had bathing facilities, of which Joe took advantage. In Richmond, Virginia, he wrote:

> *Then we went to the Sally, took a shower bath went to bed at 9 PM.*

But he spent only a fraction of his journey's nights in missions or sallies. Cleanliness was important to him, and he stayed on the alert for places where he could wash. Some were commonplace, like the jungles, as in San Luis Obipso, California,

> Went to the jungle to wash up, got a freight headed to Los Angeles.

Other places were more unusual, one of the most being in Dubuque, Iowa:

> I walked around town, washed in a horse drinking fountain, nobody saw me cause its still dark at 4:45 AM.

Between the commonplace hobo jungle and the unusual drinking fountain, there were a variety of opportunities for washing. In New Orleans,

> I jumped over the fence, landed in a baseball park, by the luck there was a water spigot in the baseball park and I washed myself.

In El Reno, Oklahoma, he wrote:

> Went to a small river (Canadian) washed my feet and face…,

and in the railroad yards in Belen, New Mexico:

> Well there is this big fire near the round house and I stayed around it and washed up.

BOARDING THE WESTBOUND

Improvising was required in Needles, California, when after a few days in the sparsely populated desert, he recorded:

> *Lost my soap, had to wash with sand and water, I walked uptown first time I washed in three days.*

Going three days without washing was unusual. Shaves and haircuts were another matter, neither being much of a priority. Joe was on the road more than a month before he had his first shave, noting:

> *Got to Brooksville, Fla at 8 AM, ate breakfast two sandwiches, 1 cup coffee, took a bath in cold water, shaved. This is September 1st and it is the first time I shaved since July 28th. Went to sleep in a tourist cabin, first nights sleep in a bed was good. Someone awakens me at 8:30 and here it was Minnie.*

Minnie was a friend from home who had moved to Florida and apparently arranged their stay in the tourist cabin. In Florida, perhaps sleeping on a bed after a month of freight cars and cots reminded Kelly of the comforts he was missing, as he accepted an offer of a truck ride to Washington, D.C., followed by a ride home to East Vandergrift. From then on, my father was on his own to visit the remaining thirty-two states and Mexico.

Men shaving at the Salvation Army.
Photograph courtesy of The Salvation Army National Archives.

After going for a month without a shave, his next two came rather quickly. In Fulton, Kentucky,

> ...an old man shaves me in the jungle, this is my third shave since July 30 and this is September 17th.

The second shave, unrecorded, may have come on September 10th in New Orleans when he

> ...went to a barbers college got a nice haircut by an expert barber.

Hobos went to barber schools for free haircuts, some barber shops and a few of the larger missions provided them, and they cut each other's hair in the jungle. In Aberdeen, South Dakota, Joe described:

> *As a I am writing this there are five other bums with me in the jungle, one bum is cutting another's hair with a comb and razor and I am in a box car writing.*

In San Francisco he noted,

> *...again to town tried to get a haircut but no free chair...*

but in Los Angeles, he reported that he *got a nice haircut* at the Midnight Mission.

Besides trying to keep himself clean and presentable, Joe attempted the same for his clothes. After using a washing machine at the dog kennel in Maryland, there would be no more machines at his disposal for the rest of the trip. Some periodic washing and replacement were necessary. In Manchester, New Hampshire, he wrote:

> *Went to jail, washed my socks and BVDs. Kelly washed his socks shirt, and some underclothes...*

and in St. Paul, Minnesota:

JOURNEY OF A DEPRESSION-ERA HOBO

...came back to mission Saturday. I washed all my clothes, took a bath.

Men washing clothes at the Salvation Army.
Photograph courtesy of The Salvation Army National Archives.

From San Francisco:

Later got a place to sleep took a bath, washed all of my clothes...

and Newark, New Jersey:

Bummed our eats in Jersey City washed all clothes in Newark.

BOARDING THE WESTBOUND

Sometimes his clothes received stronger treatment. In Fulton, Kentucky, he noted:

> ...came to the jungle, made coffee after breakfast. I boiled my two shirts washed then nice and clean, put my shirts under the sun to dry...,

and in a mission in Kansas City, Missouri:

> Read the Sunday paper till 5 o'clock, ate supper, washed my pants and shirt, got my clothes fumigated.

Men cleaning clothes in the Salvation Army.
Photograph courtesy of The Salvation Army National Archives.

After being on the road more than four months, many of his clothes were worn and needed replacing. By October, Joe noted:

> *The only thing I have on me that I had when I left home is sweater and BVDs. All the other clothes are new to me. The pair of shoes I have on are the fourth pair since I left.*

Much like his meals, Joe obtained additional clothes through bumming, chores, charity, and, on one occasion, stealing. In Spokane, Washington, he wrote:

> *I bummed two pairs of silk socks...,*

and in Hannibal, Missouri, he recorded:

> *Came to this place and asked for something to eat and they made me pull weeds. So for this pulling weeds and grass, got sit down and pair of shoes.*

From Baldwin, Florida, he noted:

> *She hands me a grass cutter and said cut all the weeds from the gate to the corner of the fence. Took about 1/2 hour to do my work. She calls me in the kitchen, gives me bacon, rice and vegetables. I ate all that. Here is where I ask her for a pair of shoes, she looks around couldn't find any, but she had an extra shirt she would give me, and I took the shirt.*

BOARDING THE WESTBOUND

Missions and sallies also made some clothing available, just about all of it pre-worn. In a Los Angeles mission he noted:

> ...got a pair of pants two pairs socks all different colors...,

and at sallies in Albuquerque, New Mexico: "got a coat" and San Luis Obispo, California: "got a big thick sweater." The items from the sallies provided protection against the cold, especially in the western and Great Lake states. In anticipation of the mountains, Joe bought some clothes in Montana:

> Went to Sheridan, Wyoming came back to Billings, went to a pool room for a while, bummed grub, got a pair of rubbers, pants, shirt, vest, and a cap, all prepared for the mountains.

JOURNEY OF A DEPRESSION-ERA HOBO

Site established for men searching for second hand shoes.
Photograph courtesy of The National Archives.

Shoes, which wore out rather quickly, were always highly sought. In Memphis he wrote:

> *Today I got a pair of secondhand shoes, all white, very sporty. It seemed the shoes attracted everybody's attention, I guess everybody had a good time looking at my shoes.*

He was willing to pay for them in North Dakota.

> *I met a kid with two pairs of shoes in Ellendale, ND, I said I would give him all the money I got for those shoes. He said how much do I have, I said 23 cents, oh that wasn't enough. Well I did have 61 cents at the time but I could spare 23 cents. So I told him I*

> *was a long way from home and I needed a pair of shoes bad. I told him I lived in Augusta, Maine, he fell for it and sold them for 23 cents.*

He had a chance to buy a coat for less than twenty-three cents in New Orleans, but passed and watched an interesting case of bartering take place for it.

> *Met a goofy guy, he had two coats, wanted to sell me one for 15 cents I didn't need a coat then a guy came by with a little dog and he trades a coat for the dog.*

Joe wasn't completely broke, not with sixty-one cents on him in Ellendale, but he didn't pay for pants in Minneapolis, the only time he stole apparel:

> *Well I went around to the pawn shops looking for pants, couldn't get any so I finally snitched a brown pair.*

Pawnshops were a source of apparel for females riding the rails, travelers without access to many of the missions and sallies Joe often used. The United States Department of Labor issued a report in 1933 focusing on the extent to which the public was unaware of how many women and girls had taken to the road. The study told of the many who had been living alone and were now jobless and homeless, others who like Joe, just wanted an adventure, and yet others who were traveling with their families.

My father noted the public's curiosity in seeing female hobos, Joe writing in Richmond, Virginia:

> *...word got around that 3 ladies were on the bum and half the people of Richmond was at the freight yards.*

Joe also described them riding in pairs in Amarillo, Texas:

> *About the time it got ready to leave there were about 35 men and two women...,*

and in Rochester, New Hampshire:

> *Right after we came out of the house we met 2 girl bums.*

The girl he described as dirty in Alabama was going alone, as was the woman he saw out west,

> *...hopped the same freight to Sandy Point, Idaho, there was a woman bum on the freight with all the men.*

While he wrote of the public's reaction to these women, Joe also reported the public's reaction to him. In Fulton, Kentucky he noted:

> *This is Saturday night, all the farmers are in town doing their Sunday shopping, and I thought they had never seen a hobo before, the way they all stared at me...,*

and Ellendale, North Dakota:

> *I tried to bum an old lady for a nickel, she got so scared she jumped about six inches off the ground and said she didn't have any money.*

His appearance often drew the attention of kids. In Wilmington, Delaware, he wrote:

> *Started for the tracks, a young boy started to yell "hobos hobos" and his Sunday teacher came along and said you shouldn't call them boys hobos, so he quit.*

And in Belen, New Mexico:

> *Went uptown and all the kids are going to school, everybody looking at me. I kept going, never paid any attention to them and I could hear them say to each other he's a bum, etc.*

Joe's fellow travelers, not the general public, once had the strongest reaction to his appearance After an eight and half hour train ride, he got off in Albuquerque, New Mexico, returning there after earlier being ordered out of town, and went to the sally. He described:

> *When I walked in the sally they asked me if I was a negro or not and I told them no, they gave me a rag to wipe first then wash. I looked into a mirror and I didn't believe it was myself, I was blacker than the*

> blackest man in Africa. It took seven batches of hot water to get my face clean and yet I wasn't very clean, had a big black streak around my eyes and it took five clean bowls of water to wash my head and hair. When I came out of the bathroom they had a special treat for me, Boston Baked Beans and coffee.

After a long train ride through the mountains, this was a welcome respite. He was well-scrubbed and well-fed, on a physical and mental break, and could reflect on living the hobo life, a life whose code advocates respectful and cooperative action.

Still, Joe did avoid some people and activities, but only those that violated some principle of responsible action. In Baldwin, Florida he wrote:

> It is 1 PM, went under shade tree got acquainted with couple other bums. One showed me a .38 gun, I thought the best for me to do was get away from anyone who carries a gun...,

and at the jungle in Fulton, Kentucky:

> couple more hobos came to jungle with pint of shine, offered me some, I refused about 1/2 hr. later 2 guys got sick from booze, lucky I didn't drink any.

Riding with Kelly on a train from Alexandria, Virginia to Richmond he wrote:

BOARDING THE WESTBOUND

> ...another bum comes in had a pint of alcohol offered us drink we refused.

While shunning people and actions he didn't like, he was very responsive to those whom he enjoyed. Joe met up with a couple of deaf men in his travels, and engaged them in the same way as he did any other hobo. In Pasco, Washington he noted:

> Went to pool hall right next to the tracks, met a deaf guy on the bum, talked on my fingers to him, everyone looks like hell at us. Rode the same car with him to next division, Wishram, I went to the jungle made some coffee, deaf guy went some other direction.

Joe went to Klamath Falls, Oregon, which he marked as "about 19 miles from the California line," then headed for California and wrote:

> By this time I was about 70 miles in Calif. from the north line, met the same deaf guy I met in Pasco, W.

He had previously met a deaf man in Memphis,

> ...came back to the jungle layed down 4 a while. I met a deaf mute talked to him 4 a while, gave me a couple cigarettes.

These two men, members of the rich and proud sub-culture of the hearing impaired, one that preserves its own history and language, were blending into another sub-culture, to another distinctive way of communicating. They were becoming hobos, living by their code, being exposed to a unique set of signs used in their private communication system.

Hobo Signs

Chapter 11
ENTERTAINMENT

Men playing checks at a Salvation Army Lodge.

Photograph courtesy of The Salvation Army National Archives.

The hobo way of life, with its absence of permanent jobs and family obligations, provided a seemingly unlimited amount of free time. It's one of the aspects most appreciated by the Texas Madman, describing it as, "a life where you are not bound by time schedules." For most people, work is a sacrifice of time, a sacrifice necessary to build a life outside of work. Hobos make no such sacrifice. In 1932, with television still years in the future and computers, video games, cell phones, and other new technology in the realm of science fiction, people, and most especially hobos, relied largely on imagination and creativity, their own resources and capabilities, to fill leisure time.

My father's accounts show he was easily entertained. Of course, when Kelly was with him he had constant companionship and, given his friend's personality, a steady stream of amusement. While in Elkridge at the Elkridge dog kennel, Joe wrote:

> So Kelly and me asked for deck of cards showed them lots of tricks. They all stared with their mouths open, girl said daddy how did they do that, daddy said you can't beat them at their own game. By the way, the girl is 17 or 18 years of age, the 2 boys come from Virginia. We are through entertaining them with cards.

Next, they turned to tutoring:

> Bring pencil and paper into action showed them how to add and multiply.

JOURNEY OF A DEPRESSION-ERA HOBO

The girl and two farm hands were apparently unschooled, not uncommon for rural children in the first few decades of the twentieth century, when parents put them to work on farms at young ages. Urban and industrial areas also saw this to a lesser degree, as some youngsters went to work early to help with household expenses. But when the hard times came, even those who were committed to education could have been denied access, with the scarcity of money causing some schools to be closed and others to reduce levels of operation. During the 1932-1933 school term, the years coinciding with Joe's trip, more than thirteen hundred schools were closed in Georgia, leaving 170,000 children without education, and eighty per cent of the children in rural Alabama had no schools at all.

After Kelly went back home, Joe continued to enjoy being around people. In a mission in Minneapolis he noted:

> *Oh I am having a good time here razzed a nutty guy had lots of fun...,*

and in New Orleans:

> *Well it is 6 PM on Sept 11 I went back to the shanty and the nutty guy was still there. We named the dog "pal", he entertained us to midnight, we laughed all the time he was around.*

Once Kelly left, Joe enjoyed fleeting personal encounters but always traveled alone. With his being on the road only a little over four months, he didn't often cross paths with any person more than once. In contrast, according to the Texas Madman, "...because the hobos cross paths with each other so often, or travel the same routes, they become each other's brothers and sisters and form their self-styled family bonds." Joe, who would be returning home to family, had only transitory dealings with fellow travelers, seeking fun and enjoyment, spending bits of time with them in basic pastimes.

On a freight from Miles City, Montana to Forsythe, he noted:

>   ...*played bummy on the freight, I dropped a dime...,*

A favorite pastime of hobos traveling in boxcars.
Photograph courtesy of The Library of Congress.

and in the Albuquerque sally:

> *...played couple games checkers.*

In Salem, Oregon he wrote:

> *...met 2 guys in the jungle with a banjo and saxophone, they played about 9 numbers...,*

and later:

> *...monkeyed around St. Louis went under the bridge, big crap game in progress, I played lost 17 cents.*

As in Las Vegas, Joe was not reluctant to participate in dice games, and they surface in varied venues during the trip. The focus seemed to be less on making money than on providing some entertainment during a dreary time. Creating some sort of entertaining diversions during those years was a necessary coping technique, and reports from this era reveal marked increases in gambling.

Joe and Kelly shot craps with railroad workers in Philadelphia:

> *At midnight the whole gang of switchmen came in made lots of loud noise and started to shoot craps. I joined them and won 30¢, then the yardmaster came around and ordered the men to work. As they went to work came back in an hour, resumed the crap game*

> and again I like a fool joined them and lost the 30 cents which I won 1 hour ago, so about 4 AM everything quiets down.

And in Baltimore:

> Kelly me and the fellow that worked in the lunch room and filling station at night and the day turn man was with us, one of them said lets shoot craps for pennies, we Ok'd it. Kelly broke the boys, 65¢ in all.

His friendly games with gains and losses of sixty-five cents, thirty cents, and seventeen cents were a contrast to the already legalized business of gambling in Las Vegas. There, Joe noted:

> ...back to this big gambling house, all you could hear in here is Your hands up and your money down, every roll is a pay roll, you lay em and we pay em...,

and:

> I saw a women with about $1,000 worth of chips playing the roulette wheel. I had 80¢ and started to play the craps, I lost 55 cents and quit.

Joe also found other ways to entertain himself. He went to movies, one in Los Angeles:

JOURNEY OF A DEPRESSION-ERA HOBO

Washed up and went to a 5¢ show at 7 o clock, this is Tuesday Oct 26, Damaged Goods was playing, came out at 8:30...,

and in El Paso:

Washed my face and went to a show, after the show I went to the sally.

In Los Angeles, he also got to a burlesque show:

...go to the Midnight Mission, took a bath, got a good haircut. I get a ticket to a Berlesk Show, went in at 6 o clock come out at 8.

The Midnight Mission, a huge facility that slept scores of men a night and fed many more during the Depression, is still serving the homeless in downtown Los Angeles in its location on South San Pedro Street. (The original site that Joe visited was destroyed in a 1971 earthquake.)

Joe's eight years of formal education helped engender a strong interest in reading, and being on the road didn't totally interrupt this. The inventory of items he had on October 2nd included four books, and he recorded stopping in libraries in Hartford, Connecticut:

sat around in the library looked over books...,

and Fort Wayne, Indiana:

> Later went to the library stayed till 8 o clock went back to the mission.

My father's affinity for reading helped to give him a pride in and curiosity about America. He took time to visit state capitol buildings in Concord, New Hampshire; Baton Rouge, Louisiana; St. Paul, Minnesota; Tallahassee, Florida; Raleigh, North Carolina; and Salem, Oregon. In Richmond he wrote:

> Went to park right along side of state capitol, and saw old capitol of Confederate States.

While in Washington, D.C. he noted:

> ...we saw the national capitol monument and other places of interest.

He missed a chance to see the capitol building in Topeka, Kansas and wrote:

> Now I am bound for St. Joseph, Mo. or Topeka. About the time I fell asleep somebody locked the door, I was in one end of the boxcar and 2 guys were in the next corner. When I thought I was in Topeka I got up and tried to get out couldn't get out, well I didn't care, went back to my corner and layed down. It is pretty cold and this car has lots of paper, made a fire in the car so I

> *could see to roll a cigarette, first thing I know the floor is starting to burn, then I put the fire out and again went to sleep. When I woke I was in Kansas City, Kan, heard a brakeman walk by and I kicked on the door and hollered for him to open the door. He did, this is Sunday morning Nov 20 1932.*

In addition to his love of reading, my father maintained his love of baseball. There were sandlot games played in communities throughout the nation during these years, games that helped the locals get their minds off the depressed times. Joe went to games in Boston:

> *...after the game had supper chewed the rag till 10 PM...,*

and Hartford:

> *...went to a park to see a baseball game after the game went to a mission.*

The 1932 World Series that held his interest was played between the New York Yankees and Chicago Cubs, with the Yankees winning in a four game sweep. Joe listened to the second game of the series, a 5-2 Yankee victory, in a radio store in Montevideo, Minnesota.

The next game, which Joe didn't mention, was one of the most famous in baseball history, the one in which Babe Ruth was said to have called his shot. Batting against Cub pitcher Charlie

Root, Ruth is alleged to have pointed to the outfield bleachers, predicting he would hit a home run on the next pitch. He did hit the home run, and controversy still persists as to whether or not he actually declared he would. Joe didn't write of listening to that game, for when Babe was homering, my father was riding freight through South Dakota. He did keep a memento of the town in which he listened to the second game of the series, pasting an ad for a Montevideo bakery on the inside cover of one of the notebooks.

Central Bakery, Montevideo, Minnesota. Inside of Joe's diary.

Joe's traveling also greatly expanded his scope of experiences. One of the most interesting was watching and helping cowboys. Riding a freight from Belen, New Mexico to El Paso, Texas he wrote:

> *I hopped it and rode till midnight in a cattle car full of fresh clean straw and I am only 115 miles north of El Paso. And I was fast asleep, they put this cattle off on a side track, I missed the part that was going to El Paso.*

JOURNEY OF A DEPRESSION-ERA HOBO

> *I finished my sleep under the blanket and I piled the straw about 3 feet high and never got up till 9 oclock. I went to the stock yards and washed my face and there are 3 cowboys on horses and about 5 big cattle dealers, they were trimming the horns on the steers. There is a big runway for the steers to run and about 10 feet is a trap, a man on the side pulls down on a cable and that causes the boards to come together and squeezes the cows belly, makes it stop very fast. 2 guys grab her horns, hold her head and the other guy uses the saw, they cut the horns too short and the blood flows out like it would out of a toy water gun. The man at the cable got tired and asked me to help him, I stayed there an hour helping him and he gave a bag of smoking tobacco.*

Joe got to experience what many kids who grew up outside of the West dreamed about in his era, being a cowboy. He had seen some earlier, in Miles City, Montana:

> *Walked up town, saw an old stagecoach used during the wild and wooly days, plenty of cowpunchers walking up the street with their horses tied.*

With all that was available for Joe both within and outside the hobo community, some of his most pleasant times came from basic conversations with the general public. In Manchester, New Hampshire he recorded:

BOARDING THE WESTBOUND

> ...got there afternoon, sat around park, met a guy and started to talk about hoboing, he looked like one, but—believe it or not he wasn't.

With a farmer in Springfield, Massachusetts:

> So we talked about traveling, he seemed interested, so did his wife and daughter...,

and a woman in Trinidad, Colorado:

> ...when I sat down to the table and started to eat 4 of her kids and herself all get lined up against the wall and form a circle. The kids varied in age from 4 to 16 and they were all very interested in my talk.

These may have been people whose circumstances would never allow them to venture far from their homes, so stories from a traveling man would be entertaining and welcome additions to conversations.

Joe talked politics in Spokane, Washington with a woman who gave him a meal in her house:

> Was a big Socialist talked to me for an hour about politics. She told me if I missed the freight to come back.

Joe's response:

> Well at 7 PM I went to the freight yards and rode an empty to Pasco, WASH.

JOURNEY OF A DEPRESSION-ERA HOBO

Socialists of that era used the suffering and fears brought on by the Depression as validation of the criticisms of capitalism and of their efforts to introduce socialism into this country.

The level of interest and belief in socialism was manifested the following month in the 1932 presidential election, when the Socialist Party candidate, Norman Thomas, received 881,951 votes. This was more than triple the amount he got as his party's candidate in 1928, back when capitalism was almost universally praised for creating the wealth and prosperity of the country. Amidst the poverty, hunger, and despair of 1932, more people began looking at socialism as an attractive alternative.

A family in Council Bluffs, Iowa, also invited him back. My father wrote:

> *I went in for supper had a darn good pork chop supper, stayed in the house till 8 oclock talking about the Depression. Pretty cold tonight, had to sleep somewhere so I went to the sally, I had an invitation for breakfast at the same house. It was too far so I didn't go.*

It is ironic that in places like Iowa, home to few Polish-Americans, Joe was accepted more fully as an American than he was back home in Vandergrift. 1932 America was heavily segregated by race, ethnicity, and religion, with each group of hyphenated Americans living primarily among themselves.

At this time, before the spread of mass communication, the country contained a series of distinct regions, all with unique accents, word usages, and ways of life. While traveling as an unkempt hobo, my father was invited into the homes of people who were likely of northern and western European heritage. In Vandergrift, there would have been scant probability of this happening, even if he were dressed in his Sunday best and was as clean-shaven and as well-scrubbed as a man could be.

But on the road, in the depths of the Depression, acceptance came more easily. His hosts sought information about conditions in other regions of the country, and the shared suffering seemed to produce feelings of greater tolerance and kinship. This suffering also produced a common villain. President Herbert Hoover bore the brunt of the frustration and anger of the American public, many of whom blamed him for causing the Depression. Others, while not holding him responsible, were upset that he didn't institute direct federal assistance to the needy. Some expressed anger vehemently, others sarcastically. The shanty towns where the homeless congregated were "Hoovervilles," newspapers used for warmth "Hoover blankets," boxcars "Hoover Pullmans," and empty pockets turned inside out "Hoover flags." Parodies mocking the man flourished, including this parody of the Twenty-third Psalm, which Joe transcribed in his diary:

23rd Psalm Up to Date

Hoover is my shepherd.

I am in want.

He makes me to lie down on park benches.

JOURNEY OF A DEPRESSION-ERA HOBO

He leadeth me beside the still factories.
He disturbeth my soul.
He leadeth me in the paths of destruction for his party's sake.
Yea, then I walk thru the valley of the shadow of depression,
I anticipate no recovery,
For Hoover is with me.
He prepareth a reduction in my salary,
In the presence of mine enemies.
He anointed my small income with taxes.
My expenses runneth over.
Surely unemployment and poverty will follow me,
All the days of the Hoover administration.

Though averse to any large-scale action to try to counter the Depression, President Hoover did cut taxes shortly after the market crash in an effort to increase purchasing power. After years of living well under a laissez-fare style of governing, people now looked for more government action, although at the time it wasn't readily apparent what should be done. Mr. Hoover's memoirs later revealed that as far back as 1925, before he became president, he had grown concerned about the rising tide of speculation. While he said nothing about it publicly, many who did openly express such concerns later said that they did so with fear and trepidation, as some who did so were called "destructionists." One banker was accused by a Wall Street spokesperson of "sandbagging American prosperity" for saying in early 1929 "if the present orgy of unrestrained speculation is not brought promptly to a halt there would be a disastrous collapse."

The somber atmosphere of the Depression was so widespread and deep that many seeking a respite from reality sought refuge in the occult. One article in the magazine Smart Set from 1935 described part of the West as "swarming with spiritualists, mediums, astrologists, and all other breeds of esoteric windjammers."

Joe met one woman who was a spiritualist, and another who insisted on telling him stories of spirits and ghosts. In Albuquerque, Joe wrote:

> *There was a lady bum in this sally, she claimed to be a spiritualist, asked me if I wanted to have my fortune told. I said yes, she told me I was going to be a Bonds man and a cattle dealer, also predicted a trip to Europe in 1939 or 40, I told her she was full of bunk, she got mad.*

Though "full of bunk", this was 1932, and the only years she mentioned were 1939, when Joe married and became a father, and 1940, the year he was killed. She would have been close to correct if she predicted European trips in 1940 to other young men, as World War II sent thousands of young Americans to Europe between 1942 and 1945. The prediction about becoming a Bonds man or cattle dealer was obviously unrealistic. Still, Joe could think about other ways of avoiding the path that led into the mills or mines. In early October he wrote:

JOURNEY OF A DEPRESSION-ERA HOBO

I think I have invented something new today might make some dough on it. It is a hickey that keeps the broom together.

Whatever it was, it earned him no dough, and neither this nor any other ideas he had kept him from the mill.

A lady bum offering to read futures surely had no shortage of willing participants in a sally filled with Depression-era bums. But a teacher in Bagdad, California had no such audience for her collection of chilling stories. Bagdad was a very small town of only a few hundred people and, Joe wrote, "only 10 kids in her school," so the teacher was probably grateful to have somebody new to talk with. After Joe chopped wood and was fed:

She made me coffee and brought some walnuts on a dish and said help yourself, she talked about spirits, ghosts, and the days of witches, oh boy me getting the shivers. It started to get dark and I wanted to go, she said not to and again she started to talk about more spooks, time went by fast, I went in at 3:30 and came out a 8 o clock.

In Joe's time, Bagdad was supported by the gold mining industry. The town was located some seven miles west of Amboy, with both lying near the rail lines and Route 66. Commissioned in 1926 to run between Chicago and Los Angeles, this celebrated road didn't originally pass near Bagdad and Amboy, but the rerouting of some of the sections in the Mojave Desert put it adjacent to these towns in 1933. Dubbed the "Mother Road" by John Steinbeck, Route 66 served as the way west for thousands of Midwesterners fleeing the Dust Bowl of the mid 1930s and seeking fresh starts in California. Today, Bagdad no longer exists—its site is barren desert.

Based upon information received at the Route 66 Museum in Barstow, California, this is where Bagdad once stood.

CHAPTER 12
FOUR CITIES, ONE DESERT

Depositors anxiously line up at a New York City Bank in 1932.
Photograph courtesy of The National Archives.

Joe was in Bagdad courtesy of the railroad cops. November 3, 1932 had proceeded like many others, with Joe riding freight. But on this day a bull told him that riding freights violated the law and threw him off, placing my father in a potentially life-threatening situation. He later wrote:

> Bulls are very tough on this Santa Fe RR. Rode 30 miles and I see him coming over the tops and I was in a lumber car, I jumped off hid in the grass, he passed me up without seeing me he kicked about 6 other guys off, when it started I hopped on again, I hid in the same lumber car, it was dark now and I thought I was safe. But 40 miles down farther he shakes the freight again, oil car about 4 cars ahead of me and I saw him putting an old man off, then he came to me. I couldn't get away nohow, flashed the light on me frisked me and said don't you know you are violating the law by riding the freights. He told me to jump off, it was going about 15 miles an hour, I told him I had my leg broken 2 months ago and if I jumped I might hurt it. Then he said it stops down here about 4 miles and it did stop, the name of the town is Bagdad, Calif. Well I climbed off, tried to sneak around and grab the front end cause I was about 10 away from the caboose, well the bull saw me walking up to the front and hollered hey you get over in that field, then he watched me until the caboose came and hopped on it.

Although that freight stopped, no others did and it soon became apparent to Joe how very difficult it was going to be to leave Bagdad and the desert. He wrote,

> *I sat around near the tracks try to catch a freight, plenty of freights going by but not one stopped or slowed down, it made me mad.*

Joe then went to the schoolhouse where he chopped wood, ate with the teacher, listened to her ghost stories, and got some bad news.

> *She said you don't have to hurry cause no freights stop here..., but he kept trying.*

> *I heard a freight come by, I started up and said Good Bye I am going to catch that freight. Well I didn't catch that freight it, went by me 50 miles per hour.*

Joe wrote in the diary the simple phrase, "now I am stranded in the desert." The words may have been simple, but the meaning was ominous. With the freights speeding by, boarding was impossible. Surrounding him was the Mojave Desert—an expanse of some 20,000 square miles that includes the site of the nation's highest recorded temperature of 134° in the shade. Bagdad itself had earlier endured a twenty-five month period of no measurable precipitation. Joe probably was unaware of this, but he knew he was in a desert and he knew he could have plenty of trouble. Told that there was a water tank twenty-two miles down the track,

BOARDING THE WESTBOUND

where freights stopped to refill their coal-heated boilers, he quickly decided:

> ...my only chance is to walk 22 miles through solid desert.

His trek to the water tank would have taken him past the tiny settlement of Siberia, which like Bagdad, no longer exists. Their sites are now merely parts of the vast Mojave. The cruelest, hottest days were gone by early November, but it was still a desert with high heat and scarce shade and water, a setting for numerous possible misfortunes. Being alone, he had no margin for error, and any accident or illness, heat-related or otherwise, could have been perilous. As Joe walked the tracks he wrote:

> I bummed 5 hot cakes, they were cold, not butter or syrup to go with em and 2 cold boiled potatoes, that is the best I could get I had to be satisfied. And now I am on my way across the desert for a 22 mile walk, I got a bottle of water, water didn't last very long and not a place in sight for more water, oh boy my mouth was dry I could hardly stand it...

> Then I came to a bridge, there was a barrel of old water, a sign on the barrel for fire only, I washed my mouth out with that water and it tasted salty and made me that much thirstier. I kept on going from 8 oclock in the morning to the next town, only 2 houses and one

JOURNEY OF A DEPRESSION-ERA HOBO

store, first thing I did drink a gallon water. I had 16¢, bought nickels worth ham and crackers and it is 4:30 in the afternoon. I filled my bottle up and waited till dark before I went up the tracks again, the store is 3 miles from the tracks.

Joe had walked the twenty-two miles along the tracks from Bagdad to the water tank, then three miles to the store. Back at the tracks near the tank, he recorded this chilling encounter, doing it rather blasely, considering the possible dangers:

On my way up the sand road I saw a snake coiled up and it started to buzz, I got a handful of stones and started to throw at the snake. I threw about 20 stones before I finally hit him, then I got a great big rock and got right on top of him and knocked his head off. I got my knife and cut his tail off, put the rattler in my pocket, when I got up in the morning at 4 oclock I lost it.

BOARDING THE WESTBOUND

Mojave Desert near Bagdad, California.

He had survived a potentially fatal encounter with what many consider the country's deadliest snake, the Mojave rattler. This creature, with venom up to ten times more toxic than any other rattlesnake, is somewhat dormant in the fall and winter seasons, fortunately for Joe.

Soon, he was back to dealing with a more familiar adversary, and focusing on leaving the desert:

> *I missed the 4 o clock on account of 2 bulls, then I had to wait for the next freight. I walked 3 miles for a drink of water, when I walked the 3 miles back I was thirsty again.*

Finally, he got some company, two fellow travelers who had been thrown off a freight in the desert and were also directed to the water tank as a place to catch another:

JOURNEY OF A DEPRESSION-ERA HOBO

At 8 o clock the freight came and at 7 o clock 2 more fellows that were kicked off, they said they walked 42 miles in 2 days. One of them was half dead, could hardly walk, very very weak, just came in the nick of time to catch the same freight I was waiting for. I walked about 1,000 feet from the water tank to make sure the bulls wouldn't see me it was going pretty fast and I don't suppose the bull could hardly catch it. After I was on for 30 miles the conductor came up the freight and I was riding the old bumpers, I saw him 2 or 3 cars away and ducked over on the side of the car. He passed me without ever seeing me but he saw the other 2 guys and told them to get off when it stopped. Well it did stop about 5 miles down the road and the conductor and the brakeman walking up each side, I jumped on the top of the car and these 2 kids didn't know what to do so I called them on the top and hid and we get to Needles safely. Right before it got to the Needles yards I jumped off and the kid that was half dead fell and hurt his knee pretty bad.

Needles, California was a larger city, and importantly, had a freight yard with a number of trains available for boarding. Joe soon left Needles for the larger cities of Arizona.

In contrast to the desolation of Bagdad, he had visited some of our country's largest cities, and would see more on his way back home. In 1932, America's five largest cities were New York, Chicago, Philadelphia, Detroit, and Los Angeles. Joe's journey took him to four of the five, omitting only Detroit, which he bypassed in his desire to get home by Christmas.

The first city he visited was, fittingly enough, the largest. New York's 1930 population of nearly seven million was more than double that of Chicago. It was the financial capital of the country, with Wall Street and the nation's largest bank deposits; its harbors were forces in international trade; communication and advertising industries were centered there; and it housed the country's premier theater district. It was, quite simply, New York.

Joe and Kelly were there for a short time, from six in the evening August 17, 1932 until 8:30 the following morning. Joe wrote:

> We landed in New York City at 6 PM, walked up Broadway and back down, we walked from 69th down to 33rd and B'Way. And at Columbus Circle at Broadway there were 3 meetings in progress: 1st, Health speaker and spiritualist, 2nd, unemployed workers, oh a big negro talking to beat all the drums in the world 3rd, Salvation Army. About 1,000 people listening to all the meetings.

The man talking "to beat all the drums in the world" could have been one of the more than a million African Americans that left the rural South for the industrialized North during the Great

Migration. This movement began when World War I created labor shortages in the large northern industrial complexes, continued as these newcomers were used as a hedge against potential unionization, and became even more necessary after quota laws drastically reduced the stream of immigrants from eastern and southern Europe.

Although the migration was driven by economics, the migrating African Americans also benefited from leaving behind the restrictive Jim Crow laws of the South. While conditions were better in the North, discrimination was still encountered both in society at large and in the workplace. Accordingly, African-American workers tended to be among the first let go in economic downturns and thus suffered tremendously in the Depression. The speaker in New York, talking with enough force and emotion "to beat all the drums in the world" could very well have been venting the anger felt by all the unemployed throughout the country.

After observing the meetings, Joe and Kelly proceeded on Broadway. My father wrote:

> *On down Broadway father 3 little kids dancing and singing at the storefront, bunch of people gather around and watch them. This happened next to the Capitol Theatre.*

The father and the kids were probably soliciting donations with their performance, perhaps to help with food and shelter. If they were good enough, they might have caught the eye of someone at the Capitol, which featured aspiring and top entertainers and had billed Bob Hope and Bing Crosby on the same day just a few months earlier.

Joe further described his trip to the city:

> So we walked up Broadway again to 63rd and it started to rain. We rushed to the park, bought a hot dog for 5 cents and a glass of lemonade free about 10 PM we went to sleep under a viaduct on a news stand, got up at 8:30 took a subway to Jersey City.

From Jersey City, Joe and Kelly headed for the country's third largest city, Philadelphia. Railroad bulls tried, without success, to delay their short jaunt:

> Now freight ready to go to Philadelphia. So now we are on our way to Phila., stopped at Trenton NJ for about 10 minutes and a bull came around and said where are youse guys going, we replied Phila. Then he said this freight does not go any farther than Trenton. We didn't believe him so we asked a conductor, he said this goes to Phila., we got on it again and now we are safe in Phila about 6 PM.

They stayed until the following evening and Joe, surprisingly, did not visit the treasured historical sites of Philadelphia, most notably Independence Hall. Instead, most of the time he spent in rail yards, both in the jungle and with railroad workers who treated them well. He recorded:

> We went to the switchman's shanty on the hump and got a cup of coffee and a place to sleep. There was about 40 men working on the hump, they showered us with sandwiches and fruits.

Philadelphia is the home of the University of Pennsylvania, whose Wharton School of Finance and Commerce conducted an annual Philadelphia unemployment survey. Wharton's industrial research department performed its 1932 survey in May of that year, three month's before Joe's visit. More telling than the numbers and percentages of unemployed was the effect this Depression was having on lives. The report showed a full thirty-six percent of families "living in distress," caused by insufficient food, insufficient clothing, insufficient heat, eviction for unpaid rent, loss of home ownership, loss of furniture, lack of medical attention, or some combination of the above.

Studies by the Philadelphia Committee for Unemployment Relief of people applying for work showed that ninety-seven percent of homeowners couldn't get loans on rapidly dwindling equities, all being far in arrears in the monthly payments and taxes. Finding cash from other sources was equally futile, as the savings of the group under study was sufficient for only several week's expenses, and just six percent were able to get cash or loans on their life insurance policies, with half losing their policies altogether.

Resources of African Americans were thought to be about half those of whites, and all families were forced to drastically reduce their standards of living.

A stark conclusion of the study was the importance of having one or more additional wage earners in the family as a protection against destitution if the principal wage earner lost his or her job.

Destitution, including the threat of destitution, was the essence of the Depression. A Philadelphia Relief Authority employee captured this with his remarks:

> *We have unemployment in every third house, it is almost like the visitation of death to the households of the Egyptians at the time of the escape of the Jews from Egypt.*

Two months later, in late October and some 2,700 miles west of Philadelphia, Joe was again in one of our five largest cities. It was Los Angeles, and once again, the ever-present bulls were near:

> *Got to Glendale, bulls flash lights into this empty car, got a light in my face. Freight ready to stop, I rode into the yard to get away from the bulls, jumped out ran through a field to the highway into LA. It is 2 oclock in the morning and I hit the city limits of LA, went under a bridge to finish the night's sleep, if I kept on walking I sure would get picked up so I played safe and*

> slept under the bridge till 7:30 AM Oct 25. Started for town, first guy I met in LA I asked him for a nickel, didn't get it. I walked about 2 miles, threw my rubbers away, ripped my pants on a barbed wire fence. Well I am now in the heart of LA.

Los Angeles was the country's fastest growing city at this time. Its population more than doubled in the 1920s, leaping over Pittsburgh, Baltimore, Boston, St. Louis, and Cleveland. The rapidly expanding motion picture industry helped fuel this influx. New discoveries of oil in Torrance and Huntington Beach, and acceleration of the agricultural and shipping industries were among other factors in this growth. The city received additional validation a few months before Joe's visit when it hosted the 1932 Summer Olympic Games. The games, like the motion pictures and radio, diverted people's attention.

If Joe needed any further escape, he found it in Los Angeles. He wrote:

> Go to the Midnight Mission, I got a ticket to a Berlesk show, went at 6 oclock. Out at 8, had a good sleep, washed again had breakfast at noon. I went to a penny cafeteria, everything one cent, young and old, ladies and men came here, I spent 12¢. Go up to Verdone St, came back to town at 4 oclock, had Beef Stew for supper, Washed up and went to a 5 cents show at 7 oclock. This is Tues Oct. 26, Damaged Goods was playing, came out at 8:30. Boy what a place this is after

> the show, SA on the corner playing hymns, about 12 in this company, played when the monkey wrapped his tail around the flagpole. Young kid about 12 years old asking for pennies, dimes, quarters, and half dollars, any of our friends got a penny they didn't need, well somebody throws a penny then he asks for a half dollar, more fun than the show. Went to the midnight mission, slept well till 6:30 AM, bought breakfast, got a pair pants and 2 pairs socks, all different colors, started for the freight yards at 10 o clock got a freight at 12 o clock.

As the Depression wore on, California became a beacon for large numbers of the country's destitute, many seeking work as migrant fruit pickers. John Steinbeck's classic novel, *The Grapes of Wrath,* superbly captured both the scope of this movement and the effect it had on individual lives. Soaring grain and produce prices in the 1920s led midwestern farmers to plow previously untilled land, land whose grasses served as a defense against the prairie winds. When the drought came in the 1930s, the winds blew away the topsoil. By 1934, significant portions of farmland in Kansas, Colorado, Oklahoma, Texas, and New Mexico had taken on a desert-like quality, their topsoil blown away in dust storms. Much of the land was rendered impossible to farm and became known as the "Dust Bowl," causing an exodus of near penniless farmers.

These farmers, along with other poverty-stricken Americans, moved into California in such large numbers that the California legislature enacted a law to penalize persons for bringing poor people into the state to live. The state's residents weren't eager to share their meager opportunities with outsiders, outsiders who would swell the labor pool and further depress wages. The United States Supreme Court overturned the law in 1941 only because it obstructed interstate commerce.

Chicago became the fourth of the five most populous cities my father visited on this trip, stopping there on his way back home. Between Los Angeles and Chicago, he also gave his journey an international flavor. In a September, 18th letter to friends he wrote:

> *You can bet your pants I am not coming back before I make 48 states and Canada will be thrown in for good measure.*

However, it wasn't Canada but Mexico that he threw in for good measure—Juarez, Mexico, across the Rio Grande from El Paso, Texas.

Relations between the United States and Mexico were not at their best in 1932. As jobs dwindled, the state of California deported hundreds of thousands of Mexican-Americans believing that their abundance somehow had something to do with the Depression. Unaffected by and probably unaware of this, Joe was excited about going south of the border.

> *Got to El Paso in the wee hours of the morning, I walked up the street and didn't have my blanket rolled up and*

it looked pretty big so a cop stops me and searches me and says you are OK, told me to go to the Sally, it is open all night. Went to bed got up at seven oclock, ate breakfast, and now I'm all excited about going over to old Mexico. I heard it was hard getting over, well I tried to go over on the 2 cent bridge but I couldn't, then I got back to town and got on a street car, paid 6 cents, got a hiding place in the middle of the trolley among all the well dressed people. The immigration officer got onto the car just as soon as it got on the other side of the Rio Grande and he looked at everybody carefully. Oh boy, my heart was in my throat, about the time he got to the middle of the car. I had my head turned towards the window, he never asked me a question. He questioned several others, I guess the reason he didn't question me cause too many standing around me. I managed to steal a seat, then about one minute later another officer enters, he looks through each and every bundle and I didn't have my bundle along so he did not bother me. I bought post cards, 3 for 5 cents, then I changed 10 cents for Mexican money, I got 25 centoros, if he gave me 10 centoros I would have been satisfied. I went to the post office and layed the cards down outside the stamp window and the Mexican money, he took a piece and gave me some change back. I walked up and down the street, took in all the sights, bought a glass of beer for 5¢ and started back to El

JOURNEY OF A DEPRESSION-ERA HOBO

Paso. I went to a restaurant, spent 15¢ for a meal, all told it cost me about 55¢ being in Mexico.

Soon after his short look into Mexico, Joe began to work his way back home. On the day after Thanksgiving, he boarded a train in De Kalb, Illinois and headed for Chicago. Chicago, often referred to as the "Second City," had a population of nearly three and a half million, less than half that of New York, but almost one and a half million more than the next largest, Philadelphia.

It was one of the nineteen cities used in a 1930 study by the Women's Bureau of the United States Department of Labor that looked specifically at women in that era. The study showed that women suffered unemployment very early in the Depression, with the rate of unemployed women in Chicago rising to seven percent by April, 1930 and soaring to twenty-four percent just nine months after that. It was further noted that foreign-born white women had the lowest unemployment rate, lower even than native white women. The unemployment rate for African-American women was a staggering fifty-eight percent compared to twenty percent of native whites and fifteen percent of foreign-born whites. This order was the same in every one of the nineteen cities examined. When employed, approximately twenty-eight percent of these women worked in the domestic and personal services industry, another twenty-eight percent in clerical occupations and nineteen percent in manufacturing. Joe's two older sisters, Marta and Jean, were foreign-born whites working as domestics and remained employed throughout the Depression in Buffalo and Newark, respectively.

Overall unemployment in Chicago was likewise high, as the large complexes in the iron and steel, meat packing, and foundry industries decreased production, small businesses were closing by the hundreds, and three quarters of the city's banks failed.

However, this was not much different than what most of the country was experiencing, and Chicago was a comfortable stop for Joe. He had lived there and still had friends, so he was treated with warmth and affection by old acquaintances, staying in relative comfort.

On the day after Thanksgiving he recorded:

> *At 12 o clock noon I caught a passenger for Chicago, still eating on the train, rode the train way down town 2 blocks from the station went up saw my old boss, asked him for street car fare, he gave me all the change he had 40¢, business rotten. Now I go up to my old roommate, glad to see me, just in time for supper, a nice big rabbit supper. I was just like a new president shaking hands all day and night, played cards, no sleep all night, sat up and talked, went to sleep in the morning at 9 AM, got up at 3, got a free haircut, free beer. I wanted to leave this is Saturday the 26th, they wouldn't let me go, drove all over town, played 500 till 2 o clock in the morning, got up at 10. Again I wanted to go, oh this is Sunday, they told me I would have bad*

luck for leaving on Sunday, rode around town Sunday afternoon and evening hours full of company, I knew them all. Played cards and danced, they wanted me to stay for a week. I told them I had to go. Went to sleep Monday morning at 2 AM, got up at 11 and at 12 o clock dinner time I left took a street car to South Chicago, waited till 5 o clock no freights, went into a caboose, ate supper with the crew, rode to Indiana Harbor, caught a freight to Niles, Mich.

Joe obviously knew many people in Chicago, and shook so many hands he felt like a new president. And there was indeed a new president in the country, as Franklin Delano Roosevelt had won the first of his four presidential elections just a few weeks earlier. Joe was well treated in Chicago, even by the railroad crew that fed him before he left for Niles. From Niles, he went to Kalamazoo, Michigan, then down through Indiana, Ohio, West Virginia, and finally back into western Pennsylvania. Leaving Chicago, he was less than two weeks from home, in time to spend Christmas with family.

Chapter 13
HOLIDAYS

Christmas day, 1932. People lined up for a meal provided by the Salvation Army in New York City. Joe, who originally planned to be on the road for Christmas, had returned home in early December.

Photograph courtesy of The Salvation Army National Archives.

Four other holidays passed while Joe traveled the rails. On Labor Day, he was in Tallahassee. This was no small day to a man from the world's steel making center, and was important throughout the country. But that year, in the depths of the Depression, the normal festivities were replaced by anger and frustration by the many who had no place to work.

The nation's first large parade in honor of labor was held in New York City on September 5, 1892, twelve years before Congress made it an official legal holiday, and an historic year in the story of organized labor. It was in this year that the famous Homestead Strike occurred near Pittsburgh. The Carnegie Steel Company brought in hundreds of armed Pinkerton guards to disperse striking workers, and on July 6, 1892 a confrontation between them left ten people dead—three guards and seven workers. Non-union workers were hired to work the mill under protection of the National Guard, one of twenty-three times in that year a National Guard unit was used to suppress union activity in various industries in states throughout the country.

But on Labor Day in 1932, Joe was on his normal search for food, and appropriately enough, had to do some work for it. He chopped wood at the Tallahassee Hotel in exchange for a meal, leading him to proclaim,

Pretty good feed for a bum on Labor Day!!

Nearly two months later, on Halloween, Joe was on the other side of the country, in Milford, Utah. He wrote:

JOURNEY OF A DEPRESSION-ERA HOBO

It is Oct 31st, Halloween, and all the store windows are marked with soap wax. And tried to get a job washing the soap off but couldn't, so I bummed potatoes, onions, bacon, carrots, and went to the old jail house and cooked up, got more sugar had a darn good dinner. After dinner, Marshall came around and said clean the ashes and the floor, that was easy, layed around till supper time, got bread, potatoes, coffee, milk, sugar and pork sausage, fried the sausage had too much for supper. Washed my feet and socks, now it is about 7 PM, walk up street, the whole town is out celebrating Halloween. They are pushing 2 farmers wagons all over town, one's a water wagon they upset it right in the middle of the main drag, and this wagon was pushed in front of a gas pump at a gasoline wagon. I followed the gang when they went to the cops house and took the toilet from the backyard on to his front porch, later I went to the dance hall, everybody having good time.

Joe had a good time on Halloween. However, what appeared to be a harmless prank of upsetting one farmer's wagon and putting another near a gasoline pump may easily have been something quite different. These were especially cruel years for farmers. In 1932 there was an abundance of crops but prices had dropped so low that many farmers felt it wasn't worth their while to even pick. Corn, for example, cost approximately eighty cents a bushel to grow but brought only ten cents a bushel in the marketplace. In this environment, farmers faced the real danger of losing their farms, and, not surprisingly, sometimes reacted with violence. With no government help or outside assistance of any kind, farmers banded among themselves to oppose bankers and government agents trying to remove families from their land. They also attempted to raise prices by restricting supply, using such means as hijacking trucks delivering food to market and actively destroying crops. Perhaps my father witnessed a harmless Halloween prank, but it might have been a farmer publicly displaying his refusal to farm; or retaliation against a farmer who did take his crops to market.

Help for farmers, and others, arrived after the 1932 election of Franklin Delano Roosevelt. Roosevelt and his advisors instituted a wide-reaching series of programs known as the New Deal, including the Agricultural Adjustment act and Farm Credit Act, that helped restore farmer's purchasing power and enabled refinancing of farm mortgages.

The Social Security Act, created to provide old-age assistance, was perhaps the most notable of the New Deal initiatives. Among the scores of others were several known by their initials: CCC (Civilian Conservation Corps), PWA, NIRA, TVA (Tennessee Valley Authority), REA, FERA, all designed to help stimulate the economy and provide relief and support for the needy. While the creation and implementation of these programs was not instantaneous, a change in the presidency restored some spirit in the country. As one business journalist noted,

JOURNEY OF A DEPRESSION-ERA HOBO

The people aren't sure just where they are going, but anywhere seems better than where they have been. In the homes, on the streets, in the offices, there was a feeling of hope reborn.

(Source: *The People's Century*)

Joe was in Winslow, Arizona on the historic election day. He wrote:

Well 3 oclock, grabbed a freight to Winslow, got to Winslow at 9 PM went to a flop house, got up at 7 AM Nov 8 1932. First thing I do is bum a bakery, got turned down then I went to the biggest cafe in town, he made me split egg boxes and take the nails out, I did that easy enough, I got hot cakes extra large and 2 eggs, 2 cups coffee and this is election day, legal holiday declared.

"This is election day" was a simple phrase, but it was a day that changed the nature of government in America. Ousted President Herbert Hoover was prophetic during his losing campaign when he declared, "This election is not a mere shift from the ins to the outs. It means deciding the direction our nation will take over a century to come." He was right, as the results of that election still influence the philosophy and policies of our government today, reflecting a change in philosophy from a hands-off, no interference style of governing to one that embraced the notion that government had a legitimate role, indeed a responsibility, in providing a reasonable quality of life for its citizenry.

On November 8, 1932, Franklin Roosevelt learned that he would be taking over the reins of the United States government. On November 8, 1932, Joe, too, had a good day, noting:

> *I made $1.40 in about 2 hours, I bummed every man in town and his brother. So now the same guys I asked before were coming back and forth, the best thing I could do is get off the street, then I went and bought meat and buns, went to the jungle made coffee ate my dinner.*

Joe had initially planned to return home in early 1933, but he still needed to travel through Michigan, Indiana, Ohio, and the northern West Virginia panhandle to see all forty-eight states. By early November out west, the cold was starting to become a problem. On the last day of October, in Milford, Utah, he wrote:

> *It is 11 PM Oct 31, 1932, oh it is cold and I got to hop a freight to California and I am in Utah.*

Heading back from California, through the mountains of the Southwest in November, the cold was bitter. In Arizona, going from Williams to Winslow, he recorded,

> *…snow on the mountains, slept next to a hot stove, up at 7 AM Nov 8, 1932.*

JOURNEY OF A DEPRESSION-ERA HOBO

The cold worsened in New Mexico:

> *I found an empty car crawled in spread my blanket and fell asleep, got to Gallup at midnight, somebody hollered at me and said get the hell out of here this is a division and they are shifting around. I didn't want to get out cause it was too darn cold; I got on at 5 o'clock, rode for four hours, too cold to ride so I got off at Las Vegas N Mex. Boy I am shaking like a leaf; The wind was cutting right through me so when it gets to Albuquerque I hopped off. I was so cold I could hardly walk, I walked like a paralyzed man.*

Finally he escaped the cold, traveling through Texas, Oklahoma, and some of the farm belt states. This route brought Joe into Illinois for Thanksgiving, spending that holiday in De Kalb:

> *Passenger train had a dead head baggage coach, I got in and rode to De Kalb, got off at 5, had running water in this car, hot and cold. This is Thanksgiving day, I went to a house got a handout, biscuits and chicken went to the jail, slept, the cops got turkey from someplace, brought it in the jail with coffee. At 8 o clock opened the door, I bummed some more to eat, first place got hand out roast beef sandwiches then the next place, I guess the biggest house in town, got a turkey*

BOARDING THE WESTBOUND

handout, cake and the trimmings of turkey, enough for 2 meals in the bag.

It was from here that Joe went to Chicago for three nights, then to Michigan and toward home. In Michigan the cold again bothered him and he noted:

Caught a freight to Niles, Mich. got there at 9 o'clock, too cold to ride, I found an old shanty, had a stove in it.

The cold also kept him from visiting Detroit, instead going through Kalamazoo, Michigan; Fort Wayne, Indiana; and Fostoria, Columbus, and Newark, Ohio on his way back home. On the last night of the journey, he stayed in Bellaire, Ohio, a city across the Ohio River from Wheeling, West Virginia.

Rode as far as Bellaire, Ohio went to jail, slept, got up at 7 AM ate the apples and cookies, started for Wheeling, had to pay 5¢ toll.

Getting to Wheeling put him in West Virginia, his forty-eighth and last state, and within one hundred miles of his East Vandergrift home.

CHAPTER 14
ADMIRING THE VIEWS

Railroad tracks alongside the Pacific Ocean between Lompoc and Santa Barbara, California. Joe rode these rails on October 24, 1932.

Joe returned to family and friends with plenty to tell. He would recount the places he visited and recall the people he met—those who made him laugh, those he felt sad for and those he admired. He would describe how people lived on the road, people with no homes and whose only possessions are what could be carried with them. His stories were captivating to his listeners back home.

In addition to all the interesting episodes, it is likely Joe wanted to convey something else that defined his trip—the wonder he felt by observing the vastness, variety, and beauty of America. While Joe used his diary primarily for recording daily living and amusing anecdotes, he did make a few notations of the train ride and surrounding scenery. In Georgia, when a freight didn't stop, he wrote:

> *This freight is the first one in 13 years that did not stop. The tower man said if he was ever reported the engineer would get fired, so we rode the passenger half way between Savannah, Ga. and Jacksonville, Florida and got off at a water tank. This is in the wilds of Georgia, all a person can see between Savannah and Jacksonville is swamps and forests. So we are stranded in this wilderness of Georgia a thousand miles from no man's land, so we have to walk 10 miles to the next station to catch a freight.*

JOURNEY OF A DEPRESSION-ERA HOBO

Joe and Kelly walked these tracks along the Georgia Pines between Everett and Thalmann on August 29, 1932.

Joe saw fascinating topography and scenery in the desert, swamp, and forest he walked through, but he didn't consider traveling by foot the ideal way for him to see the country. Trains were a great way to appreciate the landscape. They moved over the tracks at a pace at which the landscape would be seen slowly changing, granting the observer time to digest the view and anticipate what was ahead. In Trinidad, Colorado he noted:

> *The limited train came, the name of the train is "The Chief". It is the fastest train the Santa Fe owns, runs between Chicago and Los Angeles in 52 hours, I rode it for 8 1/2 hours. Before I hopped on, I wrapped paper over my feet. It made only 3 stops. What I mean this train really traveled, going over the mountains it didn't*

BOARDING THE WESTBOUND

go very fast, but once it got on the level stretch I bet it didn't go less than 65 miles per hour.

What a difference between Chicago being two days away from Los Angeles and the two hours it now is. The advantages of present day speed are undeniable, numerous and far-reaching. The business community has certainly benefited, with productivity, efficiency, maximization, and optimization all enhanced through shortening the country by lessening travel time. More importantly, many lives doubtlessly have been saved because of the speed at which we now can move, the ultimate endorsement of its benefits.

Still, something has been lost because the trip no longer takes two days. There was the sense of anticipation that builds when approaching a far away place; indeed, there were such things as far away places. When access is easy rather than difficult, when visits are commonplace rather than rare, the senses of mystique and wonder associated with travel are seriously diminished. More than revealing the continuous subtle and occasional spectacular transformation of passing scenery, the pace of rail travel seemed to present a chance to re-claim some time. Aboard the passenger trains, like the Santa Fe Chief, it was sort of a haven, removed from people demanding access to riders' time, thoughts, or emotions. The riders were afforded time to think, about where they've been, where they're going, on the train, in life.

Back on the freights, Joe took advantage of this leisurely pace, and enjoyed his ride, making note of some of what he saw. In

JOURNEY OF A DEPRESSION-ERA HOBO

the Santa Lucia mountain range, near the California coastline, he wrote:

> *This Oct 22 morning went through San Jose Paso Robles, ate my eggs and jelly roll, now it is all mountains, went through 5 tunnels, all within half mile and one about 2 miles down farther. 2 pretty U-U turns, better than the one at Altoona. Coming over the mts, 3 engines on this freight, at Gold Tree a turn is almost a perfect horseshoe, got to San Luis Obipso at 4 PM.*

After leaving San Luis Obispo, he wrote:

> *At 1 o clock freight leaving for Los Angeles, got on a good empty car. Riding near a town named Surf was the first thrill I had since riding the freights, it was going about 50 miles hour down grade and only 30 feet away the Pacific Ocean was roaring and the freight going faster, a big curve was ahead and a small bridge, I thought the train was going to plow into the ocean, but later I saw the bridge.*

BOARDING THE WESTBOUND

The bridge near Surf, California.

It wasn't as thrilling in Mississippi, where Joe wrote of riding through the Yazoo Valley:

> *Coming north from Vicksburg to Memphis is about 235 miles, and all I could see on that freight ride was cotton, cotton, and more cotton. All along the Yazoo Valley the scenery was interesting. I had a few offers to pick cotton at 50¢ a hundred lbs, but I didn't plant any, thats why I didn't pick any cotton. A good cotton picker averages 150 to 250 lbs a day, imagine what I could make picking cotton.*

He was offered a half-cent per pound to pick cotton, which in 1932 was selling for only five cents a pound, a price that likely discouraged taking it to market. His quip about not picking cotton because he didn't plant any was prophetic, as later in the

JOURNEY OF A DEPRESSION-ERA HOBO

Depression the Southern Tenant Farmers Union would strike against the cotton planters and refuse to pick. Tenant farmers were supplied land, cabins, farm equipment, fuel, and fertilizer in return for giving the landlords up to half of the crop.

This agreement, combined with the unprecedented low crop prices of the early 1930s, resulted in these farmers receiving between three and five hundred dollars in net annual income in those years.

These diary references to the scenery and ride reveal how Joe was attentive to his surroundings, and friends recalled how genuinely the overall splendor of the American landscape moved him. By his calculation, he had ridden the trains for 13,776 miles on the journey. There were obviously times when he could see nothing, but for a vast majority of his traveling time Joe was an interested spectator admiring the varied natural beauty of the country. From the trains, he could watch a constant parade of picturesque scenery, some of it subtle, some overwhelming, and see it changing from the Atlantic in the east to the Pacific in the west. Joe saw it all, the Atlantic Coastal Plains, the Appalachian Mountains, and the Great Interior Plain, which extends for more than a thousand miles from the Appalachian Highlands westward to the foothills of the Rockies.

He went through the Rockies, the Mojave Desert, the western mountain ranges, and the coastal plains along the Pacific. He saw the oceans, the Gulf of Mexico, and several of the Great Lakes. After writing "I am exploring the Miss. River from south to north," he did so, from New Orleans in the south to St. Paul, Minnesota in the north. Besides this, our greatest river, the trip had him ride alongside, stay near, or cross over most of our other important rivers, including the Hudson, Delaware, Missouri, Rio Grande, Colorado, Columbia, and Ohio.

CHAPTER 15
RETURNING HOME

The outskirts of East Vandergrift. After traveling 13,776 miles by his calculation, here Joe was within four blocks of his house.

Joe's journey came to a close along the Ohio River, in Wheeling, West Virginia, a short freight ride from East Vandergrift. In Wheeling, Joe ate in a mission for the last time, and surprisingly, this mission asked for money. While he was often asked to perform chores in numerous missions and sallies, here he wrote:

> Went to a mission, he gave me coffee and a bread. A guy next to me had a bowl of oats, I said how about bowl of oats. He gave it to me, when I started out he said you owe me 5¢ colonel, I asked him for what, he shows me a bill of fare so I had to give him 5¢.

Joe hadn't planned on ending his trip by paying for oats in a mission. He planned to end it in style. He wrote in a September 18th letter:

> So I will make Wheeling W.Va my last stop 1933. By then I expect you to send a scout to Wheeling and have him place a lb bacon and when I reach Wheeling I will pick the bacon up. Then it would be safe for me to say I will be wheeling the bacon home on wheels from Wheeling W Va. Remember and send a scout, down under the B&O bridge is where I want the bacon cached. I guess we will have to select a prominent citizen to name the scout, I hope they select Kelly. I will let you know 3 weeks before time.

JOURNEY OF A DEPRESSION-ERA HOBO

The eighth grade dropout had an exquisite alliterative phrase, "wheeling the bacon home on wheels from Wheeling." Joe, after a long absence, wanted to show he was doing his share by "bringing home the bacon", signifying putting food on the table. He didn't write a letter telling of his new arrival date, and came home without the bacon, but was home for Christmas and the cold northern winter.

From Wheeling, a Baltimore and Ohio freight took Joe to Pittsburgh, then another to East Vandergrift, just a block from his house. Friends vividly remember his feet wrapped in paper, a tactic he used to fight the cold. It was an amusing sight to the welcoming committee and a gratifying one to his parents, relieved to see that he avoided not only the cold, but all the other potential hazards of the rails.

The close of 1932 was not the best time to be thinking about a future, not with so many businesses closed, and with virtually no one being hired for permanent jobs. In better times, Joe would have had several options, such as returning to Chicago, setting up his own radio shop in East Vandergrift, or joining his father at the mill. Instead, he, along with much of the population, waited and hoped the country would emerge from the most severe Depression in its history. For the next several years, he worked in a series of short-term jobs, including semi-regularly in a friend's family radio and phonograph store. The decade's latter years brought two substantial changes for Joe. The most significant was his meeting Louise while she was working as a waitress in a North Vandergrift restaurant. The other was Joe finally getting a full-time job. Shortly after the economy regained its footing, Louise went to work at the Schenley Distillery in Schenley, Pennsylvania, some twelve miles from Vandergrift, and Joe was hired at the local mill. The man who went into the steel mill in 1938 was in many ways the same man who boarded that first freight in late July 1932. He left with a curiosity about his new country, an eagerness to see it, did so, and came back with his spirits intact. Joe maintained his uncomplaining, non-judgmental outlook, readily accepting what he saw and what befell him as just being part of life.

But there were differences, too. There was an increased confidence born of living by his wits, and a perspective that was immensely broadened through staying in every region of the country, seeing various ways of life, traditions, and people. His bank of memories was also broadened, with fond remembrances of his days on the road. The trip produced an incomparable collection of experiences, experiences his friends and family in East Vandergrift enjoyed hearing. They already had information about some of the exploits from Kelly who had been home for a few months and who had already shared some interesting tales. He had plenty of material—during his month on the road with Joe, they were arrested and sent to court in Maine, walked down Broadway in New York City, and were offered lifetime jobs in a Maryland dog kennel.

Letters and postcards that Joe sent home gave highlights of a few other episodes, and there was also the first book of his diary, mailed home from Aberdeen, South Dakota, his twenty-ninth state. In addition to recounting his activities, Joe tracked the mileage for each segment of the trip, and from Pittsburgh through Aberdeen, he noted that he had traveled 5, 279 miles on the rails. Joe's note on the last page heightened the anticipation of his return:

> *Do not copy any of this cause it only contains briefs*
> *Will enlargen when I return.*

He did "enlargen," perhaps with some embellishment, of the places he saw, the people he met, the unusual events he experienced. There was a lot of interest and there were a lot of laughs.

While aware that this wasn't the focus of his trip, his friends nonetheless correctly surmised that Joe would observe and talk with people in various regions of the country about the Depression's effects and develop some insight. He did have some informed observations that he shared with friends and family in East Vandergrift, giving them a firsthand report on conditions across American in late 1932.

It wasn't until mid-1935 that encouraging signs of an economic recovery began to appear, and not until 1937 that industrial production finally rose to pre-crash levels. Even then, the economy was still vulnerable enough that another recession took hold in late 1937 causing high levels of unemployment well into 1939. Then, in September of 1939, World War II broke out in Poland, and while the United States didn't enter until more than two years later, it had already begun producing military equipment for the British and French arms build-up, pushing industrial activity to increasingly higher levels.

BOARDING THE WESTBOUND

The economic resurgence brought Joe into the mill, starting in the United States Steel Corporation's Vandergrift plant (formerly Carnegie-Illinois), then transferring along with other less senior workers to the company's Irvin Works facility in West Mifflin. Many of his friends either began or returned to work in the mill or Vandergrift Foundry at that time, and most of them, along with his youngest brother, Zigmond, would go overseas to fight in the war a few years later. Kelly got a job in the foundry, where many East Vandergrift men worked. Much later in their lives, Joe's contemporaries would become admiringly known as the Greatest Generation, a title gained in part for having built America into the world's premier industrial and economic power, surviving the Great Depression, defeating the aggressors in World War II who sought world domination, and increasing opportunities for the less dominant ethnic, religious and racial groups.

Joe suffered his fatal accident in the slab yard of the Irvin Works a half century before those accolades were given. On December 5, 1932 the day he returned from his adventure, his life was already seventy-five percent over. He returned to East Vandergrift two months before his twenty-third birthday and was killed one month after his thirtieth, robbing him of the chance to see where his hopes and plans would take him, and removing from the world all the knowledge and experience that were uniquely his. Death came without warning, denying him the chance to say his good-byes. The accident limited his married life to barely a year, having married Louise De Michele in early 1939, and allowed him to be a father for only a matter of months, my being born in late December 1939.

Louise DeMichele at age 24 in 1938.

Joe Szalanski at age 29 in 1939.

Chapter 16
A WIFE'S MEMORIES

Joe and Louise in early 1939. This picture remained in my mother's wallet for the rest of her life.

Joe would always be in Louise's mind, a mind whose capacity grew limited in her later years. Whether it was dementia, Alzheimer's, or something else that caused this diminished performance was never officially diagnosed, but the label wasn't important. The results were the same regardless of what it was called; her capacity was what it was, as was the level of requisite care and support. Most importantly, these afflictions, whose very names can engender feelings of fear, despair, sympathy, and pity, didn't adversely affect Louise's quality of life. Somehow, seemingly miraculously, her condition brought her more than three peaceful, anxiety-free years. Impaired mental ability obviously strikes with varying degrees of intensity, with different levels of harshness and severity, but Louise couldn't have ordered a more desired state of mind. Far from receiving another cruel blow from fate, as in 1940, this peaceful, tranquil condition was the first of two kind acts of fate given at this stage of her life.

Whereas Joe kept a diary that chronicled a path traveled by very, very few, Louise was now in a lifestyle shared by a large, and growing, number of elderly

The world of Joe's diary was the whole continental United States. It was boxcars, strangers' homes, sallies, missions, and jails. Bedridden, Louise's entire physical world became a single bedroom in the house in which she lived since 1916, save for the time of her marriage in 1939 and early 1940. Her life was enhanced by a television on twenty-four hours per day, and with the ability to read thankfully intact, an around the clock reading light. With me, a lifelong bachelor, still living at home and her caregiver and friend,

Linda, seemingly always there, she never wanted for company. Regular visits from family and friends augmented this, including on one memorable occasion, a visit from several members of the Little Sisters of the Poor, an order of Catholic nuns renowned for their care of the elderly. The visit produced an oft-repeated story among the nuns who, upon leaving, told Louise that they would pray for her, asking for her prayers in return. Much to their delight, she mischievously replied that she would be charging for her efforts. For the quiet times there were magazines which were read, forgotten, and reread again and again until new ones came, and the television shows, focusing on "nice", "kind" people like Gomer Pyle, Gilligan, Steve Urkel, Edith Bunker, and Louise Jefferson.

Domenick and Angeline's eight children in 1986.
Louise is seated at the far right of the picture.

This was her life, and the memory deficiency, rather than diminish it, actually enhanced it by allowing her to believe that she was still physically active. With a new dress on everyday, she was always ready for action. Fortunately, her caregiver Linda had previously been our housekeeper, so her daily appearances led Louise to believe they were going to clean together. In my mother's mind, the daily routine also involved activities outside the house, including pushing her wheelchair-bound cousin Ralph around town and carrying chairs to picnics held in the park beyond our back yard.

With these and other feats that she was convinced that she was doing, life was pretty good, with her only awareness of needing help appearing when a diaper needed to be changed. She was coasting now, most of her life's work done, allowing others to care for her. However, she was still enlightening and entertaining to her loved ones, for, as is often the case in people with short-term memory difficulties, much of her long-term memory was intact.

My mother's family moved into the house in which we lived in the summer of 1916, before her second birthday, and she could recall events from pre-1920. She knew virtually the entire history of the family in the United States, and heard many first-hand stories of life in the country left behind, of the village of Scorciosa, and of the people, most of who would never be seen again by the new Americans.

Lying in bed, Louise would recount this history, stretching from Scorciosa to Vandergrift, where most of her family congregated and remained. There was the short stay near Harrisburg and

JOURNEY OF A DEPRESSION-ERA HOBO

Uncle Joe's return to Italy, then brothers Pete and Tom and sisters Mary and Rose joining Domenick in Vandergrift, where seven of his eight children stayed. She recalled a house filled with sounds of the Italian language, and of the Italian music flowing from the phonograph, known as the "talking machine" by the immigrants. The sounds of this language were also part of my early world, having grown up in the 1940s with two native Italians in the house, my grandmother and Uncle Tom. Uncle Tom came to this country in 1923 with the understanding he would later send for his wife. He never precisely defined what he meant by "later," and spent the remainder of his life in our house while his wife, Lucia, lived hers in Italy. It was Tom, who, when I was five years old, overheard one of my grandmother's friends compliment me on my ability to speak Italian and couldn't resist offering his unsolicited opinion, the opinion that his five year old great-nephew spoke Italian like a "Spanish Cow."

The passing of time silenced this language, brought additions to the family, and reductions. Several were taken too young, and, as with Joe, were remembered fondly by Louise. There was Uncle Pete, described by her as "a tall, good-looking man," felled by the flu epidemic of 1918, a week before his twenty-second birthday and months before his scheduled marriage. Of course, there was her father, Domenick, who suffered a fatal stroke in 1929. His memory, too, was kept alive, as Louise told of a kind, gentle man, nicknamed "Irish" for his red hair, who proudly dressed in a white shirt and tie every Sunday, and a man easily pleased and contented. Louise often repeated the story of the elation and pride he felt over something seemingly as simple as getting a new lunch bucket for his days in the coal mine. Then there was cousin Nick, who went off to the war in 1943. Right before leaving, he walked the hundred yards or so from his house to see Louise, asking her not to re-marry until he returned from the war. He never did, and she never did.

Nicholas M. Pocetti, 1925-1945.
One of America's honored fallen in World War II.

Nick's death in 1945 begat another of my early recollections, three rooms filled with adults unable to stop crying. History records the effects that wars have on countries and the world, but at age five I deeply felt the effect they can have on individual families, and sensed the boundless heartache an untimely death can precipitate.

But time was merciful, its passage reducing the sting of sad events and allowing sweet, agreeable reminisces to endure. That era of the immigrants adjusting to a new country and a new way of life remained particularly vivid for Louise. Though able to recall the passing of most family members, there was some degree of confusion and uncertainty over whether her mother and aunts Mary and Rose were still living, with her most often believing they were still with her. When her memory began to grow faulty, we decided not to be concerned about her being factually correct. Rather than let her dwell on things that could be upsetting, we emphasized keeping her happy and peaceful. She had passed enough tests in her life, and we granted her the luxury of usually being wrong. So when she would periodically declare "I haven't seen my mother in two weeks," the standard response was that Angeline was in Harrisburg helping Coomba Luigi, himself long dead. This was a very acceptable answer, because Coomba Luigi had been so good to her family, and certainly earned this assistance.

My mother's notion that Angeline and Aunts Mary and Rose were still living led to one of the more touching episodes of her bedridden, forgetful years. Her niece Maria brought a small stuffed animal for company, but thinking her mother was in Harrisburg with Coomba Luigi, Louise decided it would be nice to give the doll to Angeline upon her return. Agreeing, I bought another one for her, which she immediately designated for Aunt Rose. Leaving the room, and admiring my mother's still selfless attitude, I was interrupted by the loudest, most startling yell of her three and a quarter years of bed confinement. Fearing a medical emergency, I was surprised and relieved to discover the problem. We needed a stuffed animal for Aunt Mary, since we obviously couldn't give one to Aunt Rose and not Aunt Mary. Soon, she was sleeping with three stuffed animals, and I was assuring her daily that she had them matched up correctly—this one for her mother, that one for Aunt Rose, and the other one for Aunt Mary. These three women, still providing comfort, had been gone from earthly life a total of seventy-eight years.

JOURNEY OF A DEPRESSION-ERA HOBO

Angeline's 90th birthday party, with son John sitting next to her. It was attended by family, friends, and neighbors, many of whom, like Angeline, were Italian immigrants.

Shortly after the passing of her mother, Angeline, in the spring of 1982, Louise took her own cross-country train trip, fifty years after Joe's. Unlike him, she was a paying customer on a passenger train, traveling west to California to see her nephew David in Los Angeles and sister-in-law Marta in San Francisco. Though returning home by plane, my mother enjoyed the train ride, stopping in Chicago and Belleville, Illinois, site of the National Shrine of Our Lady of the Snows, where for decades she sent contributions in memory of Joe. After happily conversing with fellow passengers, there was still plenty of time to be alone on the nearly 3,000 mile trip, and it must have been impossible for her not to think of Joe and reflect on their time together, to wonder if he rode over those same rails, or saw the same sights.

When reminiscing with others, she was seldom heard to lament being widowed so early, telling all that Joe was a nice man, and telling me that I would have liked him.

Twenty years later, in the contentment of her room and senior years, she still reflected on their time together, but she also remembered a more distant past, when she was a young girl growing into adulthood, seeing her parents' generation change from sometimes frightened, always hopeful immigrants into genuine Americans. My mother lived through the struggles and difficulties, and developed an appreciation for their resolve and determination, and for their capabilities.

Many in Vandergrift shared this appreciation, and on Sunday, August 15, 2004, the first annual *Festa Italiano* was held in the park behind our house, the park to which Louise thought she brought chairs for picnics. This day, the Holy Day of the Assumption for the Catholic religion, began with a Mass in the park that attracted some eight hundred worshipers. More than four thousand more came throughout the day, listening to traditional Italian music, watching the folk dancers, and enjoying a variety of outstanding Italian food. The organizers strove to create a fun-filled, feel-good type of day, and succeeded, but they harbored another motive of deeper significance. They sought to honor those immigrants of the late nineteenth and early twentieth centuries, to pay respects to those who left all that was familiar and dear behind to begin anew in a strange land.

At times, those immigrants faced rejection and hostility from a less-than-welcoming citizenry. These feelings were manifested in the Congress' repeated attempts to pass a law requiring prospective immigrants to take a literacy test. The proposed test, in which aspiring immigrants would have to demonstrate an ability to read in the language of their choice, appeared non-discriminatory on the surface. In truth, the proposed law was directed at the uneducated poor from southern and eastern Europe, where illiteracy was the norm among the poor.

Several congressional attempts to limit access met presidential vetoes, first by Grover Cleveland, then William Howard Taft, and Woodrow Wilson, but congress eventually overrode a Wilson veto in 1917. The new literacy test, along with ensuing national origin and quota laws, legalized a policy toward Europeans that favored those from northern and western countries and limited the number from the south and east of Europe.

President Wilson eloquently articulated his opposition to using literacy tests as a means of gate keeping. In his veto, he wrote: "it excludes those to whom the opportunity of elementary education has been denied, without regard to their character, their purpose, or their natural capacity. In this bill it is proposed to turn away from tests of character and quality and impose tests which exclude and restrict." History, through the lives and accomplishments of the millions for whom the doors had been kept open, validated his wisdom and courage.

Rather than diminish American culture, as originally feared, our forbearers did much to preserve, advance, and enhance it. This extraordinary group is gone, but their children, some in their nineties, came to the park in Vandergrift that day for *Festa*

Italiano, as did their grandchildren and great grandchildren. They came to thank those who crossed the ocean for their foresight and perseverance, and hoped they would look down and see that their sacrifices were fruitful. The dreams that these immigrants carried ashore have largely been fulfilled.

Louise would have loved the day, but she wasn't there, not even in her imagination. Unlike Joe, she had a full life of eighty-seven years, and unlike Joe's terrible, crushing end, she died peacefully, in her house, in her bed, two years before the celebration in the park. As if in one last act of kindness, the fates allowed her to be in the presence of a loved one when she drew her final breath.

At 10:00 PM on April 7, 2002, as I brought a glass of water into the room, she leaned forward, began to smile, and then fell back as her heart stopped. She had gently boarded the Westbound, hopefully headed for the heavenly paradise in which she devoutly believed, hopefully to see Joe again, after sixty-two years.

APPENDIX I
HOBO GLOSSARY

Looking back from the rear of a train, looking back to the previous stop, then on to another, on to another state.

Hobo lingo was invariably colorful and extensive, and this is but a brief sample. Joe picked up very little given his short time riding the rails, but was well aware of it, referring to bulls, divisions, jungles, sit downs, and sallies, among other terms, in his diary.

Bulls: Railroad police.

Division: A main freight yard.

Hoover blankets: Piles of newspaper used as cover for sleeping.

Hump: A low hill in a freight yard over which train cars are pushed; also the Continental Divide.

Jungle: A hobo encampment, usually near a railyard.

Reefer: Refrigerator car.

Relievers: Well-fitting, sturdy shoes.

Riding the tops: Riding on top of the moving train cars, usually to escape the bulls.

Sally: Salvation Army mission.

Seals: Placed over freight car door locks to prevent hoboes from accessing them.

Sit down: A full meal inside a home.

Water tank: Stops in isolated areas between rail yards where train engines could take on water; a convenient spot for hobos to hop on and off trains.

West bound: What a hobo is said to catch when he passes away.

Yard bull: A railroad cop who stays in the yard rather than riding the trains.

APPENDIX II
TRIP DETAILS

Railroad bridge near Surf, California, with the Pacific Ocean on one side and an inlet on the other.

Sequence of Trip

East Vandergrift, PA;
Pittsburgh, PA;
Harrisburg, PA;
Elmira, NY;
Binghamton, NY;
Albany, NY;
Mechanicville, NY;
Boston, MA;
Manchester, NH;
Concord, NH;
Rochester, NH;
Dover, NH;
Portland, ME;
Manchester, NH;
Keene, NH;
Brattleboro, VT;
Springfield, MA;
Hartford, CT;
Providence, RI;
Bridgeport, CT;
New York, NY;
Jersey City, NJ;
Newark, NJ;
Trenton, NJ;
Philadelphia, PA;
Wilmington, DE;
Baltimore, MD;
Elkridge, MD;
Washington, DC;
Alexandria, VA;
Fredricksburg, VA;
Richmond, VA;
Raleigh, NC;
Hamlet, NC;
Charleston, SC;
Savannah, GA;
Thalman, GA;
Everett, GA;
Jacksonville, FL;
Brooksville, FL;
Tampa, FL;
Brooksville, FL;
Baldwin, FL;
Bainbridge, GA;
Tallahassee, FL;
Pensacola, FL;
Flomaton, AL;
New Orleans, LA;
Baton Rouge, LA;
Vicksburg, MS;
Memphis, TN;
Marion, AR;
Memphis TN;
Fulton, KY;

Mounds, IL;
St. Louis, MO;
Hannibal, MO;
Davenport, IA;
Dubuque, IA;
La Crosse, WI;
St. Paul, MN;
Minneapolis, MN;
Montevideo, MN;
Milbank, SD;
Aberdeen, SD;
Ellendale, ND;
Aberdeen, SD;
Mobridge, SD;
Marmarth, ND;
Miles City, MT;
Forsyth, MT;
Billings, MT;
Sheridan, WY;
Billings, MT;
Livingston, MT;
Helena, MT;
Missoula, MT;
Sandpoint, ID
Spokane, WA;
Pasco, WA;
Wish-ram, WA;

Portland, OR;
Salem, OR; Albany, OR;
Klamath Falls, OR;
Redding, CA;
Sacramento, CA;
San Francisco, CA;
Oakland, CA;
San Jose, CA;
Paso Robles, CA;
San Luis Obispo, CA;
Santa Barbara, CA;
Glendale, CA;
Los Angeles, CA;
Barstow, CA;
Yermo, CA;
Las Vegas, NV;
Caliente, NV;
Milford, UT;
Las Vegas, NV;
Barstow, CA;
Bagdad, CA;
Needles, CA;
Williams, AZ;
Winslow, AZ;
Belen, NM;
Albuquerque, NM;
Santa Fe, NM;

Las Vegas, NM;
Denver, CO;
Trinidad, CO;
Albuquerque, NM;
El Paso, TX;
Juarez, Mexico;
El Paso TX;
Tucumcari, NM;
Amarillo, TX;
El Reno, OK;
Enid, OK;
Caldwell, KS;
Kansas City, KS;
Kansas City, MO;
Leavenworth, KS;
Falls City, NE;
Omaha, NE;
Council Bluffs, IA;
Boone, IA;
De Kalb, IL;
Chicago, IL;
Niles, MI;
Kalamazoo, MI;
Ft. Wayne, IN;
Fostoria, OH;
Marion, OH;
Columbus, OH;
Newark, OH:
Bellaire, OH;
Wheeling, WV;
Pittsburgh, PA;
East Vandergrift, PA.

Railroad Lines Ridden

Pennsylvania RR;
Erie RR;
Boston and Albany;
New York,
New Haven and Hartford;
Richmond Fredricksburg Potomac:
Seaboard Line;
Louisville and Nashville;
Illinois Central;
Frisco Lines RR;
Chicago Burlington Quincy;
Chicago Milwaukee St. Paul;
Northern Pacific;
Portland and Seattle;
Union Pacific RR;
Southern Pacific;
Santa Fe (or ATSF) Rock Island Lines;
Northwestern,
Nickel Plate RR;
Michigan Central;
Chesapeake and Ohio;
Baltimore and Ohio.

1932 Dates/Locations Where Joe Slept

July 31-August 3, Unavailable

August 4, Mechanicville, NY, Jail

August 5, Freight to Boston, Moving boxcar

August 6, Boston, MA, Friend's house

August 7, Boston, MA, Friend's house

August 8, Rochester, NH, Jail

August 9, Portland, ME, Jail

August 10, Rochester, NH, Boxcar in railyards

August 11, Manchester, NH, Jail

August 12, Brattleboro, VT, Jail/Boxcar in railyards

August 13, Springfield, MA, Mission

August 14, Hartford, CT, Mission

August 15, Providence, RI, Mission

August 16, Providence, RI, Refrigerator car in railyards

August 17, New York City, Under viaduct

August 18, Philadelphia, PA, Building in railyards

August 19, Wilmington, DE, Caboose in railyards

August 20, Baltimore, MD, Salvation Army

August 21, Baltimore, MD, Friend's house

August 22, Elkridge, MD, Farmer's house

August 23, Alexandria, VA, Boxcar in railyards

August 24, Richmond, VA, Salvation Army

August 25, Richmond, VA, Boxcar in railyards

August 26, Raleigh, NC, Salvation Army

August 27, Freight to Charleston, SC, Moving boxcar

August 28, Savannah, GA, Boxcar in railyards

August 29, Thalman, GA, Boxcar in railyards

August 30, Jacksonville, FL, Mission

August 31, Jacksonville, FL, Salvation Army

September 1, Brooksville, FL, Tourist Cabin

September 2, Brooksville, FL, Tourist Cabin

September 3, Baldwin, FL, Boxcar in railyards

September 4, Freight to Bainbridge, GA, Moving boxcar

September 5, Tallahassee, FL, Boxcar in railyards

September 6, 42 miles west of Tallahassee, Sawmill

September 7, Pensacola, FL, Boxcar in railyards

September 8, Flomaton, AL, Boxcar in railyards

September 9, Freight to New Orleans, Moving boxcar

September 10, New Orleans, LA, Mission

September 11, New Orleans, LA, Mission

September 12, Freight to Baton Rouge, LA, Moving boxcar

September 13, Freight to Vicksburg, MS, Moving boxcar

September 14, Vicksburg, MS, Hobo jungle

September 15, Memphis, TN, Salvation Army

September 16, Memphis, TN, Boxcar in railyards

September 17, Freight to Fulton, KY, Moving boxcar

September 18, Freight to Mounds, IL, Moving boxcar

September 19, St. Louis, MO, Salvation Army

September 20, St. Louis MO, Under bridge

September 21, Dubuque, IA, Sandhouse

September 22, La Crosse, WI, Boxcar in railyards

September 23, Freight to St. Paul, MN, Moving boxcar

September 24, St. Paul, MN, Refrigerator car in railyards

September 25, St. Paul, MN, Mission

September 26, Minneapolis, MN, Boxcar in railyards

September 27, Minneapolis, MN, Mission

September 28, Montevideo, MN, Caboose in railyards

September 29, Millbank, SD, Building in railyards

September 30, Aberdeen, SD, Salvation Army

October 1, Aberdeen, SD, Boxcar in railyards

October 2, Freight to Mobridge, SD, Moving boxcar

October 3, Mobridge, SD, Jail

October 4, Marmarth, ND, Jail

October 5, Freight to Miles City, MT, Moving boxcar

October 6, Miles City, MT, Jail

October 7, Freight to Forsyth, MT, Moving boxcar

October 8, Freight to Billings, MTMoving boxcar

October 9, Freight to Missoula, MT, Moving boxcar

October 10, Freight to Spokane, WA Moving boxcar

October 11, Spokane, WA, Brewery used as mission

October 12, Spokane, WA, Barn

October 13, Freight to Pasco, WA, Moving boxcar

October 14, Portland, OR, Boxcar in railyards

October 15, Portland, OR, Mission

October 16, Freight to Salem, OR, Moving boxcar

October 17, Freight to Klamath Falls, OR, Moving refrigerator car

October 18, Freight to Redding, CA, Moving gondola

October 19, Freight to Sacramento, CA, Moving boxcar

October 20, San Francisco, CA, Mission

October 21, San Francisco, CA, Mission

October 22, Freight to San Luis Obispo, Moving boxcar

October 23, San Luis Obispo, CA, Salvation Army

October 24, Los Angeles, CA, Under bridge

October 25, Los Angeles, CA, Mission

October 26, Los Angeles, CA, Mission

October 27, Barstow, CA, Sand house

October 28, Freight to Las Vegas, NV, Moving boxcar

October 29, Las Vegas, NV, Jail

October 30, Las Vegas, NV, Gambling Casino

October 31, Milford, UT, Jail

November 1, Freight to Las Vegas, NV, Moving refrigerator car

November 2, Las Vegas, NV, Desert

November 3, Bagdad, CA, Abandoned boxcar

November 4, Walk through Mojave Desert from Bagdad Desert

November 5, Freight to Williams, AR, Moving boxcar

November 6, Williams, AR, Mission

November 7, Winslow, AR, Mission

November 8, Freight to Belen, NM, Moving cattle car/Boxcar

November 9, Albuquerque, NM, Salvation Army

November 10, Las Vegas, NM, Jail

November 11, Freight to Denver, CO, Moving boxcar

November 12, Albuquerque, MN, Salvation Army

November 13, Freight to Belen, NM, Moving boxcar

November 14, Freight to El Paso, TX, Moving boxcar

November 15, El Paso, TX, Salvation Army

November 16, El Paso, TX, Salvation Army

November 17, Freight to Amarillo, TX, Moving boxcar

November 18, Freight to Enid, OK, Moving boxcar

November 19, Freight to Kansas City, KN, Moving boxcar

November 20, Kansas City, MO, Mission

November 21, Omaha, NE, Salvation Army

November 22, Omaha, NE, Salvation Army

November 23, Boone, IA, Jail

November 24, De Kalb, IL, Jail

November 25, Chicago, IL, Friend's apartment

November 26, Chicago, IL, Friend's apartment

November 27, Chicago, IL, Friend's apartment

November 28, Niles, MI, Shanty in railyards

November 29, Kalamazoo, MI, Jail

November 30, Ft. Wayne, IN, Mission December 1, Marion, OH, Salvation Army

December 2, Columbus, OH, Salvation Army

December 3, Newark, OH, Jail

December 4, Bellaire, OH, Jail

Appendix III
JOE'S JOURNAL

Inside cover of Joe's journal. The "JOB" card indicated membership in the "I Won't Work" movement, organized by hobos who worked only by drifting from one casual occupation to another, never wanting a full time job.

This section contains a small sampling of pages from my father's journal, describing his activities in a cross-section of locations throughout the country. It shows his efforts to determine the number of miles he traveled by rail and his listing of all the railroad lines he had ridden, many of which were smaller regional lines that are no longer in existence.

Rather than risk losing the first notebook after it was filled with his writing, he put his trust in the U.S. Postal Service and mailed it home in early October. This gave family and friends some insight into his perspective on what he was seeing, doing, and encountering on his ride through America. They had already been apprised of some of what happened, hearing the sccount of the gifted story teller Kelly. Kelly, whose real name was John Zidek, was with Joe for one of the two months covered in the book that was sent home.

The following pages are just a glimpse into Joe's adventure across America.

The first book of Joe's journal, titled "My Hobo Trip of 1932."

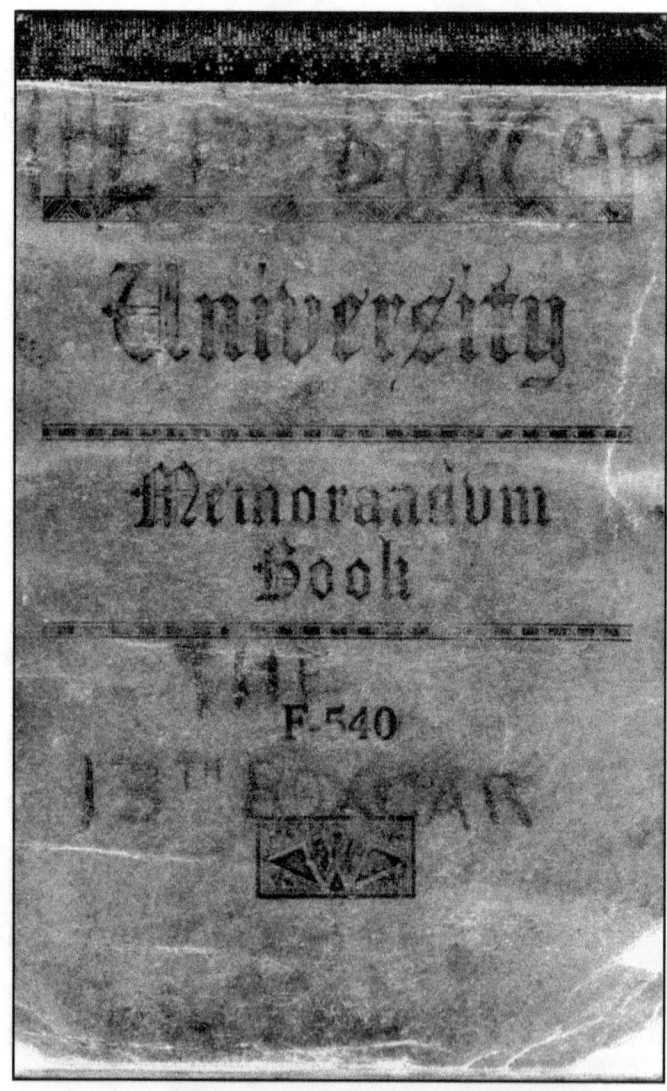
Joe's second notebook, titled "The 13th Boxcar."

Inside front cover of Joe's second journal.

men working on the hump. They showered us with sandwiches and fruits, so at 9 P.M. I fell asleep, and at midnight the whole gang of switchmen came in made lots of loud noise started to shoot craps, I joined and won 30 cents. Then the yardmaster came around and ordered the men to work, so they went to work, came back in an hour, Resumed the crap game, and again I like a fool joined again, and lost the

Playing dice with railroad workers in Philadelphia, PA.

Well we are on our way to Baltimore, got there at 4 P.M. Went to a sally, worked 2 hours, for supper and Bed. We walked around Baltimore for a while, met a couple young Kids hopping trucks, and stealing fruit, gave us apples, peaches and corn, on the cob. Well we visited Hop's place 1515 E. Fayette St. So we went to bed. Got up at 6:30 A.M. Now it is monday aug 22 -1932 Went out bummed our

Two nights in Baltimore, MD.

and got to Milford at midnight, went to the jail, and I found some cans and made coffee then went to sleep town marshall comes in at 7 in the morning wakes me up said there is a freight going my direction I didn't get up slept till eight oclock. I got some meat and onions and buns, made coffee and had breakfast in jail They have a special place in this town for bums only, this old jail had it is oct 31st, halloween and all the store windows are marked with soap and wax I tried to get a job washing the soap off, But couldent, so I bummed potatoes onions

Halloween in Milford, Utah.

to the yards, caught a freight bound towards Phoenix. Bulls are very tough on this Santa Fe RR rode some and I see him comming over the top and I was in a lumber car I jumped off hid in the grass, he passed me up without seeing me, he kicked ab'ot 4 other guys off. When it started I hopped on again, I hid on the same lumber car, it is dark now, and I thought I was safe, but 40 miles down farther he shakes the freight again, oil car about 4 cars ahead of me I saw him pulling an old man off, then he came to me, I couldn't get away no how, he flashed

Trouble with the bulls in the California desert.

and I feel just like the sunday I left home.

July 31-1932,
and I think I have invented something new to-day, might make some dough out it. It is a hickey that helps the broom together.
As I am writing this there are 5 other bums besides me in this jungle, one bum is cutting anothers hair with a comb and razor and I am in a box car writing!

Writing in his journal while in a boxcar near a hobo jungle.

> one pair socks, 1 knife, 1 comb
> Right now I have 78¢
> 2 shirts, 2 pairs pants, one cap, 2 pairs shoe strings, 2 books cigarette papers, 1 sack Dukes mixture, pair googles, new piece soap, ½ lb coffee and sugar; the only thing I have on me that I had when I left home is sweater and B.V.D's. all the other clothes are new to me. The pair of shoes I have on now are 3 weeks from the store

Some 1500 miles from home, in Aberdeen, SD, Joe makes an accounting of his assets.

in the bag, I had to throw the roast beef away. at 12 oclock noon I caught a passenger for Chicago still eating on the train. rode the train way down town 2 blocks from the station. went up saw my old Boss, asked him for street car fare he gave me all the change he had a Business rotten. now I go up to my old room mate, glad to see me just in time for supper, a nice big Rabbit supper. I was just like a new president shaking hands all day and night. played cards no sleep all night sat up and talked went to sleep in the morning at 9 AM got up at 3. got a full haircut

Seeing old friends in Chicago, IL.

Now I am stranded on the desert went to sleep at 9 oclock and I got picked off at 8:30, I found a good reefer, crawled in and slept til 2 oclock somebody comes around and said what the hell do you call this I said nothing, then he said when you get out close the doors like they were, about 5 minutes later while I was wrapping my blanket a little kid comes along saw me, went round and told the 10 other people that live in this town of Bagdad that there is a bum sleeping in a car, they all come by and look at me, so the last one came

Stranded in the desert in Bagdad, CA.

as I jumped off, I met 4 guys
they told me to watch myself
around these yards, cause the
bull just beat 4 of them up. He
almost broke one guys back,
destroyed anothers clothes,
well these 4 guys are going to
arrest this bull, they were
in the yards trying to catch
the freight I was on and that
is when the bull caught them.
I jumped over a fence, landed
in a baseball park. By luck
there was a water spicet

Getting warned about tough bulls in New Orleans, LA.

bath, went to sleep at 9 P.M.
got up at 6 A.M, wrote a letter,
ate breakfast, Started 4 Marion
ark, on my way Bummed cakes
and Bananas, got to Marion at
11 A.M ate dinner at a house got a
sit down, started back to memphis
got to Memphis O.K. Bummed a
good supper, mostly cakes today
Comming north from Vicksburg
to Memphis it is about 235 miles
and all I could see on that
fright ride was cotton, cotton
and more cotton. all along the

Riding through Mississippi cotton fields.

Yazoo Valley, the scenery was interesting. I had a few offers made to pick cotton, at 50 cents a hundred lbs. But I didn't plant any. That's why I didn't pick cotton. A good cotton picker averages 150 to 250 lbs a day, imagine what I would earn picking cotton. Today I got a pair of second hand shoes. They are golf shoes all white, very sporty. It seems the shoes attracted every body's attention. I guess everybody had a

Deciding not to pick cotton.

go under the car. I walked to a coal yard, went a little way looked into a box car there was a 40 year old guy did the childact I went up town, walked into a restaurant asked the manager for a bite to eat, He said no, So a big hearted customer said set down lad take any thing you want. I took hot cakes and sirup. coffee I thanked him. bummed a few cigarette. went to a butcher shop got about 2 lbs boloney. walked into a baker shop, asked for something,

Getting fed in LaCrossee, Wisconsin.

23D. psalm up to date.
Hoover is my Shepherd,
I am in want.
He makes me to lie down on
park benches;
He leadeth me beside the
still factories.
He disturbeth my soul.
He leadeth me in the paths
of destruction for his party's sake.
Yea, then I walk thru the
valley of the shadow of
depression,
I anticipate no recovery.
For Hoover is with me

Parody of the 23rd Palm.

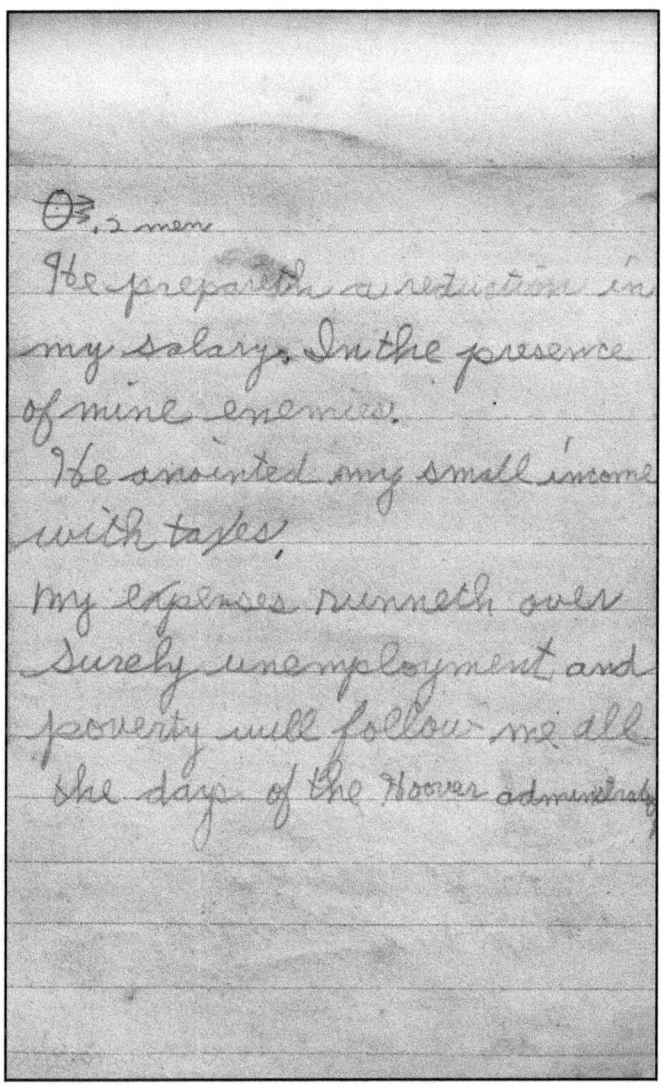

O, 2 men

He prepareth a reduction in my salary, In the presence of mine enemies.

He anointed my small income with taxes.

My expenses runneth over

Surely unemployment and poverty will follow me all the days of the Hoover administration

Continuation of the Parody of the 23rd Palm.

Mileage chart

Pitts. to Harrisburg   205
Harrisburg to Elmira   174
Elmira to Binghamton   57
Binghamton to Albany   141
Albany to Boston   172
Boston to Nashua   40
Nashua to Portland   119
Portland to Concord   89
Concord to Brattleboro   68
Brattleboro to Hartford   99
Hartford to Provid.   82
Providence to N.Y.C.   210
N.Y.C. to Newark   10
Newark to Phila.   85

Keeping track of his mileage.

1581 →

Phila to Balt.   140
Balti to Richmond   116
Richmond to Raleigh   167
Raleigh to Charl-   348
Charleston to Savanh   126
Savanh to Jacksnvll   155
Jxvll to Tampa   199
Tampa to Baldwin   179
Baldwin to Tallahssa   175
Tallahssa to New Orleans 447
N Olean to B Rouge   113
Baton Rge to Vicksburg   119
Vick to Memphis   232
Memphis to St Paul   923

Continuation of mileage computation.

> st. ~~Dubuque~~
> st. Paul aberdeen 259
>   and back
> aberdeen to Ellendale 100
>
> total miles 5279
> This is as close as I
> could possibly get. You
> know this is unofficial
> Yours will be official
> So keep on using your mileage
> chart. I just wanted
> to have an idea of mine.
> But this isent wrong
> very much.

Joe's first journal was filled while he was in Aberdeen, South Dakota. He mailed the journal home, advising friends that the chart they were keeping based upon postcards detailing his itinerary would be the official mileage chart.

```
                              7355
                    return
Billings to Sheridan        185
St. Paul to Spokane        1505
Spokane to Portland         377
Portland - Frisco           776
Frisco - Los Angeles        452
Los Angeles to Las Vegas    334
Las Vegas to Milford        243
Milford to Barstow          437
Barstow to Needles          156
Needles to Williams         261
Williams to Santa Fe        445
Santa Fe to Trinidad        224
Trinidad to Denver          180
Denver to El Paso           655
El Paso to El Reno          712
El Reno to Kansas City      000
El Reno to Kansas City      270
Kansas City to Omaha        203
```

Monitoring his mileage from St. Paul, Minnesota, including his side trip from Billings, Montana to Sheridan, Wyoming and back.

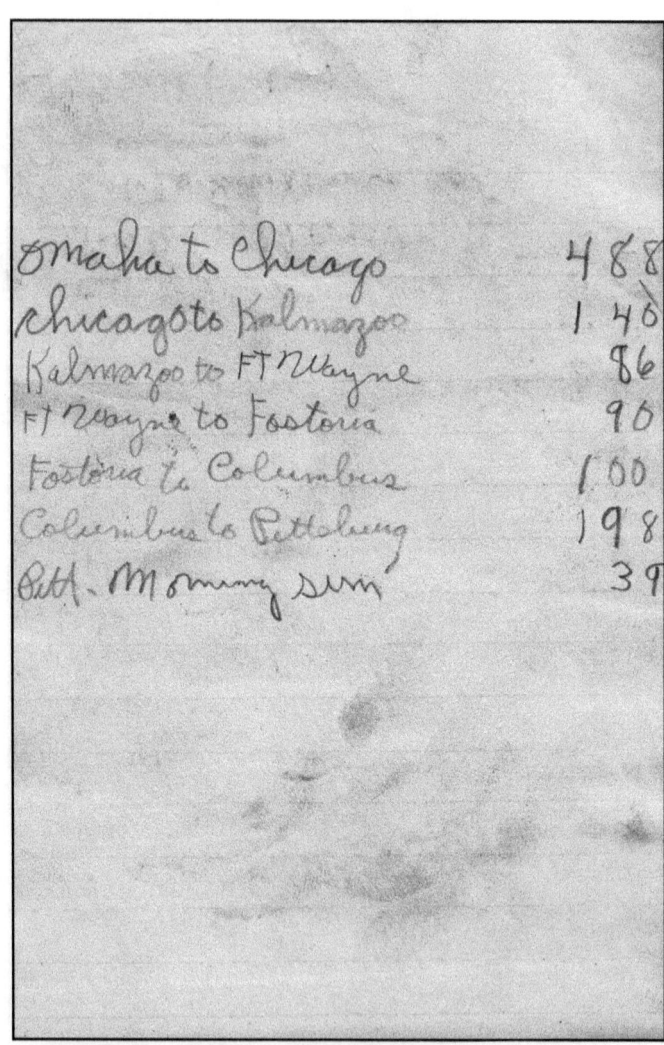

Morning Sun was home. This meant Joe's adventure was over, 13,776 miles of railroad tracks and 47 states behind him. He was home with family and friends, on to the next phase of his life, on to the final seven years of an abbreviated life.

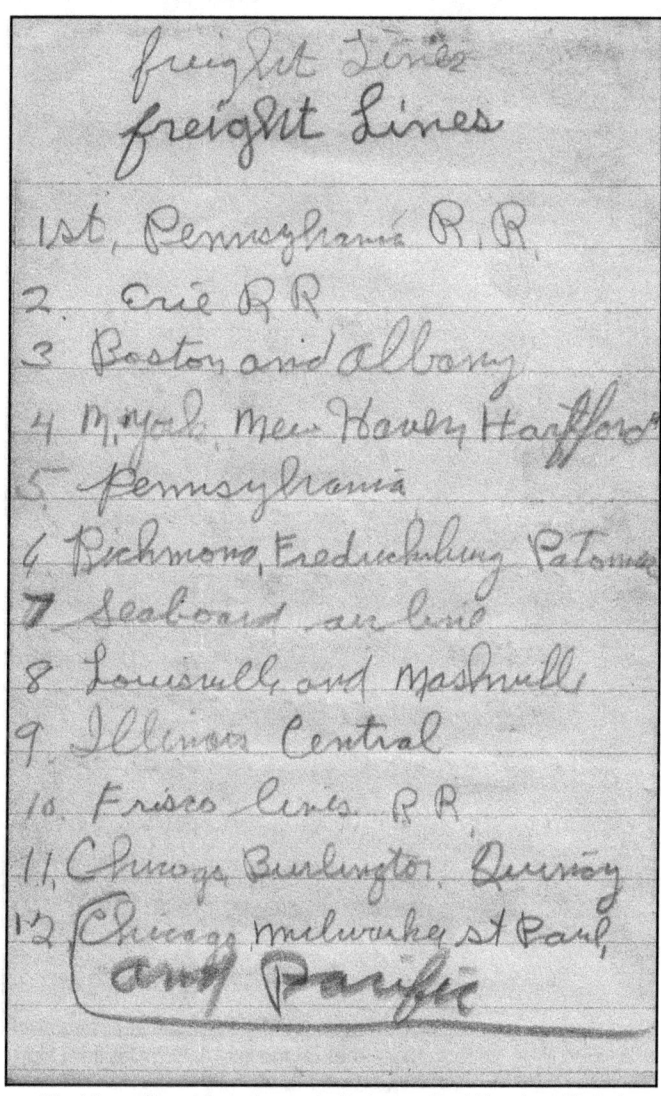

All of the railroad lines Joe rode between East Vandergrift and Aberdeen, South Dakota.

Northern Pacific RR
Spokane Portland and Seattle RR
Southern Pacific RP
Union Pacific RR
Santa Fe or A.T.S.F RR
Rock Island Line RR
Northwestern RR
Michigan Central
Nickel Plate RR
Chesapeake and Ohio RR
Baltimore and Ohio RR

Rairoad lines. He rode these lines on the final 8,496 miles from trip.

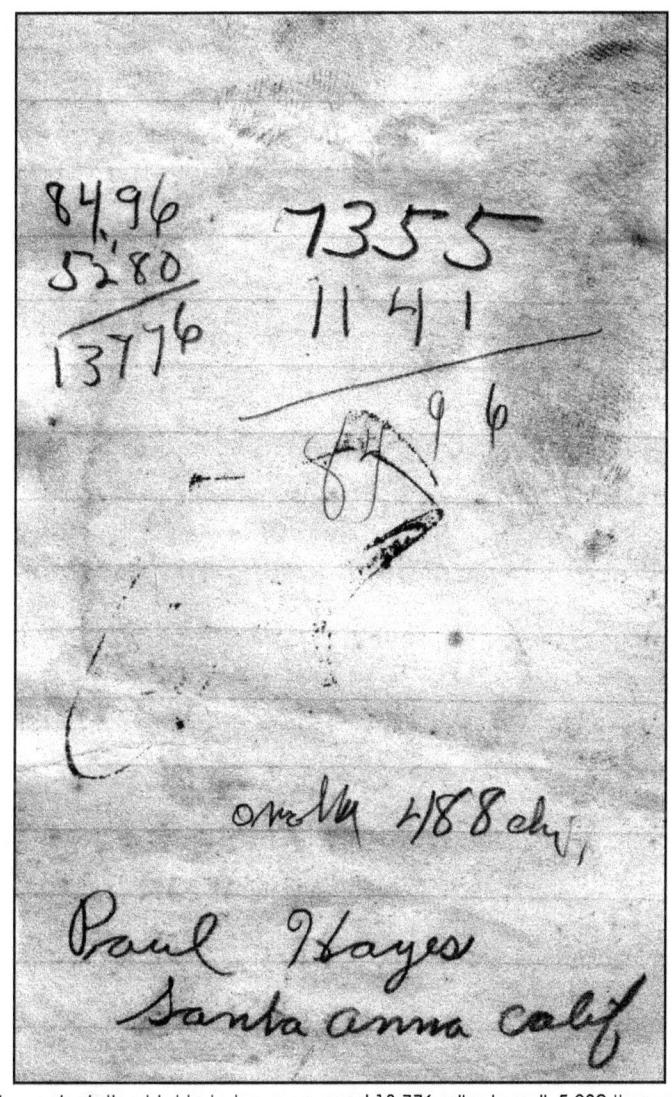

Joe calculating his trip to have covered 13,776 miles by rail, 5,280 through Aberdeen, SD and 8,496 from Aberdeen, out west and back home.

Acknowledgments

Part of the town lies adjacent to the railroad tracks and Joe would have ridden past hundreds and hundreds of such towns.

Although I had read through my father's journals several times years ago, I had forgotten about them until cleaning out some drawers following the death of my mother. In comparing their lives, hers long, his short, I thought it would be befitting to re-introduce him to the world, largely through his own writings that diligently recorded his excursion through America.

Writing this book was a gratifying experience, an experience made more enjoyable by people who not only provided me assistance, but shared my enthusiasm for this project. At the outset, there was Sam Hazo of the International Poetry Forum, who generously agreed to read the first three chapters as I sought validation and a credible opinion as to whether I should continue. It was his genuine interest and approval that propelled me to continue writing and seeking out people who would help on various subjects that would be covered.

In Chronological order, I met with:

Steve Kecman of United Steel Workers Local 2227, the union that serves workers of the Irvin Works. Steve, who lost two relatives in fatal accidents at the Irvin Works, was active in having the monument bearing the names of my father and two of his cousins created and placed near the plant gate. He also provided me with information on the operations of the plant, and with introductions to officers and staff at the union's building on Phillip Murray Drive in West Mifflin, all of whom were helpful.

Ron Baraff—Director of Museum Collections and Archives Rivers of Steel Heritage Area in the Bost Building in Homestead, PA. Ron furnished some history of the steel industry during the late 19th and 20th centuries, along with pictures that were used in the book.

Beth Caporali—Museum Director of the Victorian Vandergrift Historical Society and Museum, on Sherman Avenue in Vandergrift. Beth and her staff supplied details on the founding of Vandergrift, and the early days of its steel mill, and pictures for this book.

Linda Hughes—The Hobo Foundation in Britt, IA—Furnished information of hobo life, and photographs, including the one that served as the inspiration for the title of this book, the Hobo Cemetery where "friends who caught the Westbound" are laid to rest.

Scott Bedio-Archivest—The Salvation Army National Archives and Research Center in Alexandria, VA. Made available their collection of Depression-era photographs showing the Salvation Army providing food and shelter for the hungry and homeless during these years, many of which made excellent additions to this book.

In addition to the information and photographs received from the afore-mentioned professionals, I was able to check my understanding of family history with my Uncle Albert and Aunts Julia, Ann and Adele. To them, my gratitude extends far beyond the scope of this book.

Bibliography

The tracks are just lying there, enticing anyone with wander-lust to ride them somewhere, anywhere.

The Columbia History of the World
Harper and Row, Publishers
New York Evanston San Francisco London

The Peoples' Century
Time Books New York, NY
Division of Random House, Inc.

The Century
Doubleday
A division of Bantam Doubleday Dell Publishing Group, Inc.
1540 Broadway
New York, NY

The 20th Century "An Illustrated History of Our Lives and Times"
J G Press, Inc.
455 Somerset Avenue
North Dighton, MA

Behind the Mask of Chivalry
Nancy MacLean
Oxford University Press
New York Oxford

Something Better Than the Best
1995 Vandergrift Centennial Committee, Inc.
The Victorian Vandergrift Museum and Historical Society
Vandergrift, PA

Britt Hobo Guide
Britt News-Tribune
Britt, IA

Steelworkers in America
David Brody
Harvard University Press
Cambridge, MA

Handbook of Labor Statistics, 1936 Edition
United States Department of Labor, Bulletin No. 616
United states Government Printing Office
Washington, DC

U.S. Department of Labor, Women's Bureau
Bulletin No. 113 by Mary Elizabeth Pidgeon
United States Government Printing Office
Washington, DC

Knights of the Road
Roger Bruns
Meuthen, Inc.
New York, NY

The Great Crash, 1929
John Kenneth Galbraith
Houghton Mifflin Company
215 Park Avenue South
New York, NY 10003

About the Author
JOE SZALANSKI

Author, Joseph Szalanski

Joseph D. Szalanski, a lifelong resident of Vandergrift, graduated from Vandergrift High School and earned degrees from Holy Cross College and the University of Chicago. After working for some of Pittsburgh's major industrial firms, he formed his own small company that concentrated in helping the unemployed either re-enter the labor force or enter it for the first time. The company worked with a diverse clientele that ranged from white collar workers to displaced Kentucky coal miners and Pennsylvanian steel workers to long-term welfare recipients in our inner-cities. Now retired, he remains interested and involved in the plight of the urban poor, having written several unpublished papers for agencies that deal with the problems and prospects of this segment of our population.

WA

www.ingramcontent.com/pod-product-compliance
Lightning Source LLC
Chambersburg PA
CBHW071652090426
42738CB00009B/1498